Becoming Human
A Social Task

Karl König in Föhrenbühl in 1964

Becoming Human
A Social Task

The Threefold Social Order

Karl König

Edited by Richard Steel

Floris Books

Karl König Archive, Vol. 8
Subject: Social questions

Karl König's collected works are issued by
the Karl König Archive, Aberdeen
in co-operation with the Ita Wegman Institute
for Basic Research into Anthroposophy, Arlesheim

Translated from German by Carlotta Dyson

First published in German in 2010 under the title
Mensch unter Mensch werden by Verlag Freies Geistesleben
First published in English by Floris Books in 2011

British Library CIP Data available

ISBN 978-086315-809-4

Printed in Great Britain
by Bell & Bain Ltd, Glasgow

Mixed Sources
Product group from well-managed
forests and other controlled sources
www.fsc.org Cert no. TT-COC-002769
© 1996 Forest Stewardship Council
FSC

Contents

Editorial Note   9

Introduction *by Richard Steel*   11

Motifs of the Social Mission in Karl König's Life
   by Richard Steel   19

The Threefold Social Order

The Historical Context of the Threefold Social Order
   and the Disintegration of Europe   47
   First Lecture. Föhrenbühl, Monday, March 2, 1964

The Failure of New Social Endeavours: Meditative
   Images for a Deeper Understanding of the
   Principle of Threefolding   59
   Second Lecture. Brachenreuthe, Sunday, March 8, 1964

The Spiritual Dimension of Human Development:
   The Higher Senses as a Social Legacy   73
   Third Lecture. Föhrenbühl, Palm Sunday, March 22, 1964

Wonder, Compassion and Conscience:
   The New Garments of Christ   87
   Fourth Lecture. Föhrenbühl, Easter Sunday, March 29, 1964

Developing Responsibility in the Social Realm: A Lecture
   on the Anniversary of Rudolf Steiner's Death   101
   Fifth Lecture. Föhrenbühl, Easter Monday, March 30, 1964

Michaelmas and the Threefold Social Order

The Spiritual History of Central Europe and the
    Threefold Structure of Karlstejn Castle   115
    First Lecture. Föhrenbühl, Sunday, September 20, 1964

The Michael Festival as a New Festival of Community:
    In Memory of Rudolf Steiner's Last Address   131
    Second Lecture. Föhrenbühl, Monday, September 28, 1964

Temple Building and Community Building:
    Goetheanism and the Goetheanum   143
    Third Lecture. Föhrenbühl, Tuesday, September 29, 1964

Appendix

    The Social Organism is Threefold   161
    (Undated manuscript in English, probably 1944)

    Report on the journey to Bohemia   167
    (Notes for a travel report, Föhrenbühl, September 13, 1964)

Notes   173
Bibliography   177
Index   181

Could we not take up something of the true task of
Europe and transform it into a seed in such a way that
some of its true mission might be salvaged? Some of its
humanity, its inner freedom, its love of peace and its dig-
nity? If this were possible, might life and work not have
meaning again? Should we not try to realize something
of this Europe that has now been forced into invisibility?
To realize it not in words but in deeds? To serve and not
to rule, to help and not to coerce, to love and not to hurt.
This shall be our calling.

Karl König[1]

Karl König, Alix Roth und Carlo Pietzner in Karlsbad (Karlovy Vary) in front of the institute of Dr Brabinek, September 1964. See Appendix for König's report of the journey.

Editorial Note

The texts reproduced here are based on lecture transcripts unrevised by the lecturer, and the individual lectures and addresses had not originally been given titles. The overviews given in the table of contents have been devised by the editor as a guide to the reader.

Early on in the development of the Camphill movement, Karl König had to reconcile himself to the fact that such transcripts would be reproduced and distributed to an ever-widening circle of interested people. There was a strong desire amongst his listeners to study this material and to continue working with it. Any manuscripts destined for actual publication at the time were carefully revised by him. However, he was only able to do this for a limited number of manuscripts. As a result we are dealing here with notes taken during the lectures or with transcripts of tape recordings. We owe thanks to a small number of König's friends and co-workers, who would often create and reproduce these manuscripts by working through the night, and getting them ready for distribution by the following day! It was of course inevitable — given the standard of technology at the time — that gaps and errors have crept in. Those responsible for König's literary legacy believe that by making these texts available to a wider public with only minor stylistic and grammatical changes while maintaining the feeling of directness and immediacy of his diction, they are acting in accordance with his intentions. This also means that readers are invited to share the responsibility for the way these texts are handled. From our side we hope to satisfy the needs of readers by providing textual and factual commentary and through making the widest possible variety of archive material available. I thank Carlotta Dyson for her commitment to this work while translating.

Introduction

The lectures gathered together here were held by Karl König less than two years before his death. The fact that they arose at such a late stage in his life appears to contain a particular key to Karl König's biography and to the way he experienced his life task; after all, he had not only occupied himself with social questions and problems throughout his life but had engaged with them practically and with the endeavour to bring about social renewal, motivated by a deep historical conscience. In a certain sense these vivid descriptions which he gave during a period of six months may appear as the culmination of his life work. They bear witness on the one hand to the comprehensive way he had occupied himself with Rudolf Steiner's answers to the steadily escalating decay of Europe, on the other hand to his intense experiences with his own efforts in the realm of community building. This latter concern finds expression time and again in these lectures as expressed, for example, in this sentence: 'The essential thing is this: that we realize more and more that peace, peace among humanity, can only arise when insight is gained into the new spirituality which imbues the society, the community life of human beings.'[2]

One significant aspect that emerges very clearly from these lectures is that Karl König had gained a core insight through his own biography. Through carrying and even bearing the suffering entailed in a strong community-building endeavour he realized that something new that had long been anticipated in the social life of humanity and which had been attempted through many and diverse endeavours, cannot be 'implemented' by way of a 'programme,' even if it is born from the sincerest belief or the deepest insight. König himself was well versed in the shaping of social processes and forms; yet his main energy, his concern, and time and again his despair focused on facilitating a maturation of insight in a sufficient number of people in order to awaken in them the necessary enthusiasm for what would be required for social renewal. Latterly he realized ever more strongly that new forms of human encounter can only arise authentically from the relationship that each individual has to the spiritual realm. Through its integrating effect on the soul, this can in turn promote coherence in social processes. History had shown that from the smallest to the largest unit the noblest endeavours for social structures (and many of them were by no means *that* noble, as König describes in the first lectures), stand or fall by the way they are taken up by the individual, and which personal interests motivate them in so doing; that is, by a process of self-realization and self-mastery within the context of conscious relationships.

In the development of social forms for the Camphill communities, the practical details of daily life were never a matter of indifference to König; out of the spirit of anthroposophy everything, in particular the practical things of life, right down to the handling of money, was to be structured in a new way if at all possible. When, in 1965, he was asked for a student magazine to describe the social tasks that the Camphill communities had set themselves, he described the endeavour in this spirit:

> None of the work done is remunerated and yet everyone
> — whether he works or produces more or less — enjoys
> a livelihood appropriate for him. He works for the others
> and they for him. Mutual trust provides the basis for this
> significant social experiment. We are conscious of the fact
> that we are only at the beginning of these endeavours.
> They require us not to think in terms of implementing

a rigid system ... The fundamental principle, that
work has nothing, nothing whatsoever, to do with
remuneration, must never be circumvented ... Once this
separation has been achieved, the gradual introduction
of the threefold social order may be attempted. Without
these fundamentals, such an endeavour would never be
successful, as the coupling of work and remuneration
militates against the organic separation of the three
spheres of social life — the free, independent cultural
life, the rights sphere and the economic system.[3]

Yet he was ever conscious of the danger of falling into the
'Robert-Owen-trap.' As Rudolf Steiner describes in his fundamental writings about social renewal, and especially at the hand of
the biography of Robert Owen, success can never be achieved by
merely creating model social institutions.[4] Admittedly, Owen's
brilliant community endeavours, his dedication to the welfare of
the workers, the children and to enhancing the social and economic context of a group of people living and working together,
were in themselves exemplary. As replicable social models,
however, they were too dependent on the presence of their
'inventor.' Although contributing to a heightened awareness
of injustice and exploitation in the social and economic field,
and to stimulating similar pioneering work, one factor was not
taken into account: Owen had not reckoned with the personal
development of the individual. This dimension of development,
however, is indispensable for any authentic social progress and
for the sustainable implementation of social structures that take
account of individual freedom.

In the early years of the movement for social threefolding it
was clear to Rudolf Steiner that progress could not be confined
to the one-off creation of a new social order. Appropriate social
forms would have to be created out of the prevailing chaos insofar as this was historically possible; moreover, success would
depend on people's preparedness to pursue a new direction —

one that would also include the personal development of the individual human being. Ultimately it was just this understanding and commitment that proved to be lacking.

In this context, the establishment of the Waldorf School as the tangible fruit of Rudolf Steiner's efforts on behalf of social renewal, gains a deeper meaning. He had invested great hopes in its human foundations, in the development of the capacities of the free individuality. Karl König also took this as his immediate starting point for community building, both in curative education and in social therapy.

König was always intent on making a contribution to a common future-orientated vision in co-operation with specific, spiritually striving people, collaborating in the context of an intentional community. We may perhaps call this aim a 'realistic utopia.' Realistic in the sense that the starting point is always the actual given circumstances — the social as well as the prevailing human constellation. At the same time, however, he displayed a 'utopian' attitude in both cases. His contemporaries expressly describe a particular gift he had, connected with his commitment to medicine and curative education: in the immediacy of the human encounter, he could begin to discern the other person's path of destiny and development, helping them to recognize and follow this path. He was at all times able to carry in his consciousness the utopian element pertaining to society and the development of humanity and to translate it into a guiding principle for everyday action; he had cultivated this attitude throughout his life, against the background of global political developments. Later he had been able to intensify and focus this capacity through the study of anthroposophy.

König underlined the following passage of an article by Rudolf Steiner in a copy of the magazine, *Das Goetheanum,* referring the formation of the General Anthroposophical Society at the Christmas Foundation Meeting in 1923. Highlighting this passage, König perhaps revealed the basis for what was to become his commitment in joining the Anthroposophical Society:

[The Anthroposophical Society] will endeavour to fulfil this task [of the cultivation of a science of the spirit] in such a way that it will make its focal point the anthroposophical spiritual science cultivated at the Goetheanum with its results for brotherliness in human social life, for the moral and religious as well as for artistic and general spiritual life in the human being ... Anthroposophy as cultivated at the Goetheanum leads to results ... They can lead to a social life truly built on brotherly love.[5]

Karl König committed himself unconditionally to the promotion of this social life that was intended to be prepared 'out of the spirit' through anthroposophy. He saw a concrete possibility of realizing these future aims 'experimentally' in the establishment of communities in the context of the Camphill movement, literally as intended in the article quoted above, or figuratively as a seed, as he identified it in his essay on 'Significance and Value of the Work of Curative Education.'[6] In this context 'experimental' implies creating and establishing a living prototype or example, thereby creating transition spaces for developmental transformation.

The two cycles of lectures being published in this volume can be seen in this context. They arose from Karl König's final period of activity. In the spring of 1964 he moved from his Scottish exile to the Camphill Farming and School Community of Brachenreuthe near Überlingen on Lake Constance. In 1963 the nearby Residential Special School of Föhrenbühl near Heiligenberg had been started as an extension. This beautifully situated estate, which was ideally suited to the celebration of festivals, was not only capable of accommodating a larger number of people — children in need of care as well as their carers — but it also seemed to offer a perfect context for König himself. After casting a glimpse into the deserted festival hall he declared, 'This is just right for my lectures!'

Eventually this came to pass. He had become more and more in demand as a lecturer, travelling throughout Germany and abroad. The 'umbilical cord' connecting him back to the continent of Europe had become re-established and he needed a place from which he could elaborate on issues and themes regarding the tasks of Europe, which were so close to his heart. Apart from the co-workers from the two educational institutions, increasing numbers of people attended from the surrounding area and also from further afield to listen to his lectures. The festive opening of the School in Föhrenbühl, which he had helped to organize, took place between the two lecture cycles — at Whitsun, May 7, 1964. His subsequent brief illness and sudden death terminated this activity on March 27, 1966, in the midst of plans for lecture tours, particularly in response to invitations by the universities of Dresden and Leipzig, as well as to Prague, Budapest and Vienna.

He was particularly looking forward to revisiting the 'heart of Europe,' as he had once called the area around Prague, and the bridge to the East. In his notes of these journeys we find several striking sentences:

> Bohemia as the heart of Central Europe.
> The desire to visit Bohemia, Prague, once again was great.
> The Silesian-Bohemian destiny.
> An initial narrow chink in the door to the East.[7]

We may ask, where did that strong motivation to take hold of social conditions with such conviction and enthusiasm come from — frequently in the face of strong opposition? Why, having oriented his whole life's work towards this task, was it only in the final years of his life that he spoke so explicitly and concretely about the threefold social order? These questions will be considered in the brief biography which follows, but the reader may perhaps discover the answers for himself through the lectures published in this volume. The short essay included as an appendix, entitled 'The Social Organism is Threefold,' could be considered an early attempt; we can experience König wrestling with questions and turning to the threefold social order as a possible solution. The essay is undated; by looking at other essays — for example one addressing the relationship between his own social endeavours and the Christian Community — and through the nature of the concepts employed here as well as in diary entries around this time, we may surmise that it dates from 1944.

Perhaps without having consciously intended this, these lectures given at Lake Constance are shaped in such a way that the first five given at Easter and the other three at Michaelmas of the same year strongly incorporate these two festivals of the year, enhancing their theme in the context of the festivals. In this way, König offers us an example of practising something else that was close to his heart: to include in one's experience of any festival the one occurring at the opposite time of year. At Easter we may become seekers of the spirit under the guidance of Michael, thus preparing the corresponding festival dedicated to the renewal of the social realm. By contrast, in autumn, at Michaelmas, as we enter the dark period of the year, we may be strengthened by the power of the Resurrection of Easter.[8]

König wanted his contributions to be received as a stimulus for one's own work and especially for individual practice; because it is only when we strive towards the real consequences of becoming human that healthy social life will be possible.[9]

Richard Steel
Karl König Archive

Motifs of the Social Mission in Karl König's Life

Richard Steel

Any biographical sketch of Karl König would miss its essential point if it failed to take account of the leitmotif of his social mission. The reader who wishes to undertake a more detailed study of this motif is invited to consult König's several penetrating biographies that are part of the Karl König Archive publications.[1] In order to show Karl König as a person of social feeling and action in the context of the lectures published here, we will now take up this theme.

Deep-seated powers of compassion and social conscience are already revealed in the young boy in Vienna, although he did not have any substantial means at his disposal. Due to an accident suffered by his grandfather, his subsequent need for care and the move of the family to the city on the Danube, an already precarious financial situation was strained still further. Then came the First World War with famines and the collapse in the value of the currency. The boy was so moved by the conditions he perceived in the city which were so much worse, that time and again he spontaneously gave away his clothes. The memoirs of his mother refer to this in a heartfelt way: thus we can read descriptions of friends and family remarking on his shabby appearance. His mother could only reply, 'It is his will and there is nothing we can do about it.' In her opinion this had improved by the time he was fifteen years old; however, he began instead to give away his pocket money in the street. The inscription he had read above the entrance to the hospital on his way to school soon became a reality in his life, 'As you did it to one of the least of these my brethren, you did it to me.' (Matt. 25:40).

We can feel moved by the fact that it was just these words of the Christ which König — now towards the end of his life's journey — placed in the foreground on Easter Sunday 1964 (see p. 83). In this we can experience a human being who, having been born into Judaism, trod a very individual path, and who throughout his life has wrestled with the highest aims of modern Christian ethics. From an early age his quest frequently entailed a battle between his own mighty urges and his weak physical constitution. Very early on he became aware in himself of the need for self-development and the overcoming of inner hindrances — in the first instance his impatience and choleric tendency. His mother pictures this with Viennese charm and humour: 'Often he could get very angry, and then we would say, *"Klane Heferln gehen bald über!"* (Small jugs soon overflow).'[2] Early on he could see how much commitment and work this would entail, and soon he endeavoured to put this striving into effect in the service of his fellow human beings. While still a student he began to treat a circle of patients (homeopathically) in his parental home. His mother became aware of one particular gift, enhanced through his intensive study of anthroposophy and equally intensive inner work, which he was able to use in a healing and socially formative way throughout his entire subsequent life: 'He had his own method. Also he was able to read the psychological state of a person from his features. This meant that I could not hide anything from him ...'[3]

We are able to trace this faculty in many testimonies from contemporaries and former patients; it also guided the course of his own life through the immediate experience of the soul-spiritual qualities of another person, a landscape, or even a situation in time. Nowadays we would probably describe this as a strong gift of empathy, which in his case, however, was coupled with an immediacy of conscience. This frequently led directly to decisions, to actions — to a 'therapeutic' intervention. Inevitably his fellow human beings would occasionally experience this as an infringement of their freedom. Yet König upheld one fundamental principle from the beginning, particularly in the community building initiatives of the Camphill era: a deep respect for the autonomy and developmental potential of the individual, that is, for free spiritual-cultural life. König was always painfully conscious of the fact that he could be mistaken at times, in particular with respect to his expectations of other people.[4]

A compassionate Central European heart

It may have been this way of experiencing the world, speaking directly to the will and inducing him to engage, which touched the sixteen-year-old when he experienced concretely and at close quarters the disintegration of the Austrian monarchy, a state comprising many diverse peoples. On the one hand the experience of collapse, of unfulfilled — and even missed — historical opportunities were experienced as a burden which became imprinted in his physiognomy, which often appeared melancholic. On the other hand, his temperament — which was liable to be experienced as choleric, bearing witness to his inner strength and intensity — was directed ever more consciously towards these historic tasks that were crying out to be addressed. He identified himself with these challenges and later dedicated the emerging Camphill community to them.

What was motivating him was by no means a nationalistic feeling of loss, or merely a sense of mission confined to the political and social upheavals in Europe. It could perhaps be indicated by the broader concept of 'historic conscience.' König experienced himself as placed within a context heavy with the destiny of humanity. König implicitly experienced anthroposophy as an launching ground for social renewal, yet the anthroposophical movement had not been able to engage sufficiently with the transformation of prevailing social conditions. By referring to the 'salvaging' of something of a Central European task, König was clearly speaking from his personal sense of historic conscience. As early as 1948, when a Dutch youth group visited him during the summer recess, looking for a stimulus for their work, he chose to speak to them on the theme 'Michaelic community and the essential streams of anthroposophic life.' In a notebook we find the following preparatory entry, which bears witness to his deep connection to the threefold social order: 'The threefold social order, the light of anthroposophy, shone into the darkness, and the darkness comprehended it not.'[5]

From the very start this Christian aspect represented for König the background for all his endeavours — community as a path towards the Christianizing of the human being and the earth itself. He had to marvel at providence when he subsequently discovered — after he had already begun the work on the Camphill Estate in northeast Scotland — that the name 'Camphill' originated with the order of the Knights Templar, whose northernmost and perhaps historically last area of activity had been in those surroundings, even on that very spot itself. This was something that Karl König was able to meet time and again in his encounter with people and with landscapes: the direct manifestation of the soul-spiritual element in its destiny-shaping power. In this case he became conscious of it only afterwards. In his esoteric community building work in the Camphill movement, which had been given this name because of the Templar connection, he linked into a statement by Rudolf Steiner about the Templar Order (which, looked at superficially, had failed):

> But more and more the longing for a complete
> Christianizing of the rich treasure of the wisdom of

the cosmos and of earth evolution, for a complete Christianizing of earthly life broke through, a Christianizing of ordinary life in such a way that the sufferings of the earth, the pain of the earth and the grief of the earth appear as the rose symbol of the cross.

Time and again in people inspired in this way, in whom lived on what was meant to be annihilated through the burning of the Knights Templar, there lived the high ideal that what brings quarrel and discord should be replaced by something that can bring the good to earth, the good which can be imagined as the symbol of the cross entwined by the roses.[6]

This lecture, part of a cycle about the spiritual significance of Central Europe, was given during the First World War on Karl König's fourteenth birthday.

Picking up the thread

In addition to the outer failure of the movement for the threefold social order and the scant influence of the new spiritual science on the civilization of the age, Karl König could not but experience the failure of anthroposophy, due to *internal* social difficulties, as a personal trial. He was to experience this not merely as a spectator, but suffered under it in a very real way personally.[7] In the course of his life he had had to flee several times and to make a new beginning out of nothing, experiencing both inner and outer exile in the process. This provided one more reason and — in view of the outer circumstances — perhaps also an opportunity to start with the inner aspect, the concrete relationship between one human being and another as a path of development. What better teacher could there be in this respect than the person 'in need of special care,' with whom and for whom life-sharing situations were to be established?[8]

Developing an eye for questions of destiny certainly forms part of the path of development for anyone wanting to engage in curative education and social therapy on the basis of anthroposophy. Developing a particular inner attitude concerning questions of unfulfilled deeper intentions, intentions that cannot be realized is also called for, an attitude that those in need of care are certainly able to convey. One may come to a deep inner awareness of this reality — not in a speculative way, but by practising open-mindedness. Such a sacred, healing attitude may be capable of encompassing the future in such a way that we may begin to sense those endeavours of destiny that do not reveal themselves in any obvious way. Perhaps it is only through such selfless devotion that we discover how much of our own intentions — equally hidden and unfulfilled — meet us in the person we are caring for: shared intentions, in other words. This attitude of soul certainly moved Karl König inwardly and came to expression in many ways. In the context of his biography the way he studied historic personalities makes sense when considered precisely from this point of view: he was of course interested in history and was continually engaged in historical studies — but his purpose was always to discover the intentions of the people concerned, to grasp their significance for the present and to encompass their possible metamorphoses for the future with his own intentions.

As early as 1936–38 this had been a strong motif in his work with the young friends in Vienna, immediately prior to their mutual commitment to meet up again in some as yet unspecified location after their escape, for the purpose of founding a community in the spirit of the archangel Michael. He studied Rudolf Steiner's fiery 'Address to the Young People' with them, as well as the destinies of those fallen in the war:

> We chose as our first theme of study the works and
> biographies of individuals who had died early on in the
> World War ... We sensed that these young people

had attempted to prepare the ground for something we should continue.[9]

During the course of subsequent years König wrote a considerable number of short biographies (published as *At the Threshold of the Modern Age*) which, seen in this light, appear as of more than 'merely historical' interest. In his years in Scotland he proposed concrete tasks and working methods for small groups of people who were to take up specific inner work to support the new community-building endeavour. He allocated to each group a kind of 'patron,' a personality to whom one might find and inner connection. Among them were Raphael, John the Baptist and Francis of Assisi. For one group who had chosen as their task the cultivation of a bridge to those who had died, he mentioned Robert Owen. Morwenna Bucknall, who had been a member of the Camphill Youth Group, herself the daughter of an English social reformer, expressed disappointment, wondering what could possibly to be expected from a man who had actually been a failure. Had not Rudolf Steiner referred to him as a negative example? Karl König's indignant reply was, 'Perhaps it is a matter of what you might be able to do *for him!'*

This example illustrates how König himself tried to build bridges to the dead, appealing to others to join in the task. On the other hand he also explicitly included the dead as helpers who would be able to work in a different way from the 'other side,' having left the earthly conditions that had constricted them. Words formulated for an obituary to a co-worker who had died young became a veritable life motto for many people in the Camphill settlements:

> A social organism can only thrive and develop if the dead become part of it; if we consciously include their help and guidance.[10]

Candles, sparks and flames

König felt an overriding commitment to the high aims for humanity as carried by Rudolf Steiner and by Ita Wegman, his medical collaborator. To the latter he felt a particular personal closeness. In the case of Steiner his feelings were tinged with the bitter sense of his own omission, as despite plenty of opportunity he had never actually met him. Or might this actually have strengthened his resolve to continue his task? Undaunted and very consciously Karl König carried those resolves which in that sense had yet to come to manifestation. With strong will power, he was able to transmit these to a considerable number of people through his lectures, through the conduct of his daily life, making possible 'an awakening through the experience of the soul-spiritual being' of the other person. It becomes clear that the experience which had awakened in him a sense of his own life task — meeting children in need of special care on that first Sunday in Advent with Ita Wegman in Arlesheim — was here entering a completely new dimension. It was an experience that he often liked to relate in later years, and which, in the form of the 'Candle on the Hill,' became emblematic of the social island that had arisen in the darkness of Europe on the hill named 'Camphill.' It was a moment of intense experience of his own destiny when he realized: 'Yes, this is my future task! To awaken in each of these children their own spirit light which would lead them to their humanity, this is what I want to do!'[11]

In retrospect it can be ascertained that in the course of his life the transformative effect of his task was not confined to the destiny of those being cared for but extended to members of his audiences and to his co-workers. The broader social dimension of the 'candle experience' becomes clear, being an enhancement of what König describes in the following lectures as the path of social development: awakening through the experience of the soul-spiritual being of the other person. During the last weeks of his life, Rudolf Steiner formulated in a verse something like an archetype of this fire of enthusiasm for the big task, a fire that can jump across to the other person; a verse which seems like a special legacy and which — uniquely in his rich output of verses — begins with the word 'I' referring to himself:

> I would light every human being
> From the fire of the cosmos,
> So that he may become flame,
> Unfolding the fiery nature of his being.
> Others would like
> To take water from the cosmos,
> Which would quench the flames
> And in a watery way
> Would inwardly paralyse all being.
> Oh joy, when the human flame
> Blazes even where it rests!
> Oh bitterness, when the human being
> Remains bound where it would be active.[12]

The child of Europe

In contemplating the life and photographs of Karl König the question occasionally arises: Was he really that melancholic, even depressed? This is not so easy to ascertain. He never broke down under the multiplicity of self-imposed tasks and demands, although he inevitably experienced the depths of the darkness and the unattainability of his aims, At many points in his biography one might have expected the burden to have become too great for his vulnerable physical constitution. This would probably have been the case had it not been for his capacity to draw strength from other sources. Special experiences — or encounters — always occurred at such points.

For those of us who did not have the opportunity of meeting Karl König during his life, his most beautiful gift of this nature is perhaps the simple, pictorial description, which he called *A Christmas Story*. While it is obviously set during the Christmas season, its inner gesture is an Easter experience — moving from loneliness and despair through death to an intimation of resurrection. Initially one may be puzzled by the fact that as König, in this story, enters the Land of Resurrection and of Life, he gazes upon the landscape and poses the question: 'Has Austria died too?' The central encounter in this story is with Kaspar Hauser. This is nothing thought-out, but a deep experience in the darkness of the soul, looking for an inner Christmas; the 'Child of Europe' appeared to him — although he had long 'known' that this being has to do with the developing work of curative education. At the end of 1945 Karl König's mission of therapeutic community building again appeared clearly in connection with the failed task — with the frustrated destiny — of Central Europe. At the beginning of the war in 1918, as he sat alone in front of a candle, the Christmas experience awakened on a new level:

> Could we not take up a part of Europe's true destiny
> and transform it into a seed, so that something of its
> original mission could be rescued? A part of its humanity,
> inner freedom, love of peace and its dignity? If this were
> possible, surely we had a reason to live and work again.
> Could we not try to establish something of this vanishing
> Europe? To realize this through deeds, not words? To
> serve and not rule, to help, not force, to love and not
> hurt. That will be our task.[13]

König states explicitly that this is a task intimately connected with Rudolf Steiner's attempts at the realization of the threefold social order. For himself, however, it is particularly connected with the task of overcoming the 'inertia of the heart,' in the sense of the 'Spirit-Fire' verse quoted above.[14]

Preliminary steps towards Camphill

Although König had missed the opportunity of meeting Rudolf Steiner personally, he soon recognized a 'spiritual affinity.' Through the close relationship which he developed to Ita Wegman, appointed by Rudolf Steiner as the leader of the Medical Section of the School of Spiritual Science at the Goetheanum in Dornach, — *through* her, as it were — he was able to link into Steiner's spiritual being and intentions in a special way. In this way he experienced a confirmation of his own endeavour to pursue the therapeutic task and the social question together. In fact it was his quest for the realization of Christian community building in this spirit that initially induced him to leave Ita Wegman's side and to move away from Arlesheim to Silesia. His future wife, Mathilde Maasberg (known as Tilla), came from a long and still socially strong tradition of the Moravian Brotherhood in Gnadenfrei, a community established by Count Zinzendorf. In a letter to Tilla he expressed how strongly all this shone out for him from the human soul element in this community as well as from its surrounding landscape: he had experienced the brief meeting as the redemption of his own question of destiny. And so König began with, among others, Albrecht Strohschein, who had participated in the Curative Education Course with Rudolf Steiner, to build up the newly established home for children in need of special care at Schloss Pilgramshain.

The connection to Ita Wegman remained strong as they both shared the mission of social renewal in the Christian spirit. In September 1930, for example, Ita Wegman announced a study week for carers and social workers 'under the leadership of Dr Bockholt and Dr König.' In the lecture he gave during this conference he spoke very clearly about the connection between threefoldness in the human organism and in social organization:

> The knowledge of reincarnation and karma and their
> expression in the human organization, which Rudolf

Steiner has recognized as a threefold one according to head, chest and metabolism, is a primary foundation for all social activity.

The lecture closed with the words:

People active in social life will only be able to carry out socially upbuilding work when they are able to see the individual human being in the image of the heart and when they are able to awaken in themselves the forces working in the heart, which are in reality the forces of the living Christ working in the earthly realm. This needs to be recognized and this recognition needs to flow into each individual action carried out in the social realm. Then healing forces will be active in these deeds.[15]

This thread seems to lead directly to his later expositions in 1964 published in this volume.

When Ita Wegman invited the relatively young König to participate in her Association for Social Assistance it was probably out of recognition of his engagement with social issues.[16] Certain events were organized at that time in key places — particularly in Hamburg and Berlin — that, amidst the general mood of resurgence, were intended to point to new directions out of anthroposophy. Here he was able to renew his connection with Walter Johannes Stein, a prominent student of Steiner's, who became well known as a lecturer in the movement for social threefolding immediately after the war. During their childhood they had already met in the streets of Vienna, and Stein, too, emigrated to Britain before the Second World War. The topicality of the issues addressed, full of taboos at that time, is shown in a note by König for his lecture about 'Social Tasks of the Art of Healing' in March 1930 in Berlin.

König felt a strong need to work with Ita Wegman. However, in the face of his sense of impending political developments, he felt an even greater urge to proceed more intensely and concretely

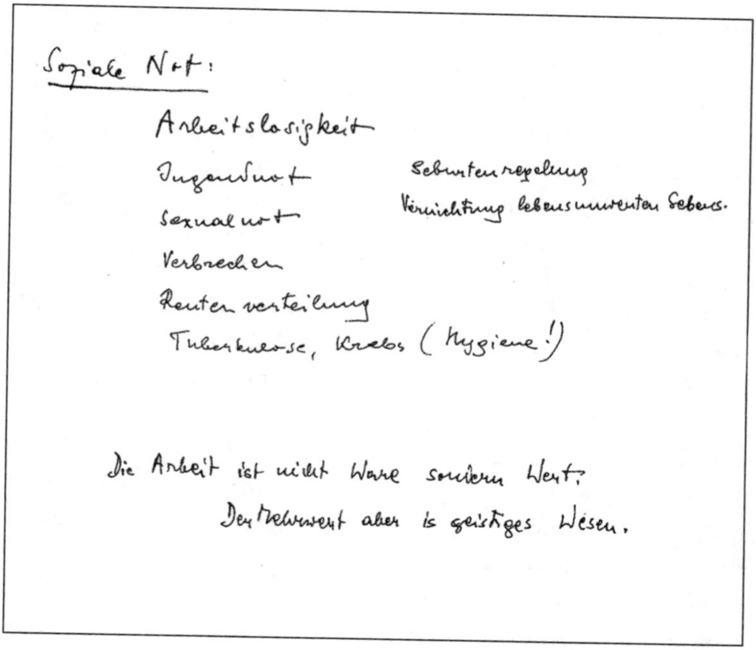
Soziale Not:

Arbeitslosigkeit
Jugendnot
Sexualnot
Verbrechen
Rentenverteilung
Tuberkulose, Krebs (Hygiene!)

Geburtenregelung
Vernichtung lebensunwerten Lebens.

Die Arbeit ist nicht Ware sondern Wert;
Der Mehrwert aber is geistiges Wesen.

Social afflictions:

unemployment
distress of the youth
sexual distress
crime
distribution of wealth
tuberculosis, cancer (hygiene!)

birth control
elimination of life not worth living

Labour is not a commodity but an asset
growth of assets arises through the spirit

Note for lecture about 'Social Tasks of the Art of Healing' in March 1930 in Berlin.
(At the next lecture he also added the theme of drug abuse)

into social work. And so he set off — not always with the blessing of Ita Wegman — on his own initiative and with disregard for the growing dangers, to give further lectures and courses in the cities of Central Europe. In addition he was pursuing the ideal of establishing the work on a Christian-religious basis. And so at Whitsun 1932, together with Emil Bock, one of the pioneers of the Christian Community, the movement for religious renewal, he founded the Independent College for Social Work. It was probably due to his sensitivity for the spiritual aura of the landscape that this foundation took place in Eisenach, not far from the Wartburg. There, in the *Sängerkrieg,* the minstrel contest, in the battle against the forces of darkness, against Klingsor, the legend of Parzival had been sung for the first time by Wolfram von Eschenbach. It is the place where St Elisabeth of Hungary had lived 700 years earlier and where in 1522 Luther translated the Bible into German.

When in October 1932 the first newsletter of the College was sent out, the opening conference and two weekend courses had already taken place. The *Letitwort* (leading thought) by Friedrich Doldinger on the cover, as well as the article by Karl König, bear witness to the fact that this attempt to address social distress arose

Opposite: The first newsletter of the College

The most urgent issue of social care, providing meaning and context for all other endeavours in this realm, is to create the necessary conditions for enabling a free and vigorous spiritual-cultural life to thrive, including a renewal of the scientific sphere, the art of education as well as artistic and religious life. Anyone who commits himself wholeheartedly to this can be sure to find himself standing in the very place where the destiny of the world is decided; he can furthermore be confident that his work will be no less fruitful in the long run than the loving care given by a social worker or nurse can be in the immediate present. To be able to offer the right stimulus may often be necessary to enable the work of social care to achieve maximum effectiveness.

Dr Friedrich Doldinger

Rundbrief

der Freien Schule für soziale Arbeit

Nummer 1	Eisenach	Oktober 1932

Leitwort:

„Die allerdringlichste soziale Fürsorge, durch die alle andere erst Sinn und Wurzel bekommt, ist: für ein freies stoßkräftiges Geistesleben zu sorgen, für eine geistgemäße Erneuerung des Wissenschaftsbetriebes, der Erziehungskunst, des künstlerischen und religiösen Lebens sich einzusetzen. Jeder, der dies wirklich mit dem Einsatz seines ganzen Menschen tut, darf sicher sein, daß er an der Stelle steht, wo das Schicksal der Welt entschieden wird; er darf auch sicher sein, daß seine Arbeit nicht weniger gute Folgen in der Zukunft haben wird, als es die liebevolle Tätigkeit etwa einer sozialen Fürsorgeschwester oder eines Krankenpflegers unmittelbar schon haben können. Rechte Anregungen geben zu können, wird oft wichtig sein, um die soziale Fürsorge erst recht fruchtbar zu machen."

Dr. Friedrich Doldinger.

Zeit-
Krankheiten

Oeffentliche Tagung

von Sonntag, den 27. November
bis Dienstag, den 29. November 1932

veranstaltet von der

**Allgemeinen
Sozialen Hilfe E. V.**

unter Mitwirkung der

Medizinischen Sektion
am Goetheanum, Dornach/Schweiz

Berlin, Brüdervereinshaus
W 62, Kurfürsten-Straße 115-116

Eintrittskarten:

	Hint. Pl. RM	Vord. Pl. RM	Studierende geg. Gutsch. RM
Einzelvortrag	0.75	1.50	0.30
Gesamttagungskarten	3.75	5.50	1.—
Erwerbslose freiwilliger Beitrag			

Vorverkauf:

Bote u. Bock, Wertheim, Bücherstube für freies Geistesleben, Potsdamerstr. 112 b, sowie an der Kasse

Auskunft

durch die

Allgemeine Soziale Hilfe E. V.
Berlin W 62, Schillstr. 11 a'''
Fernsprecher: B 5 Barbarossa 5182

Buchdruckerei Neugebauer, S 42, Oitschiner Str. 64 — F1 0158.

Sonntag, den 27. November

11⁰⁰ Dr. W. J. Stein
**Das Heilen in den
verschiedenen Zeitepochen**

Montag, den 28. November

4⁰⁰ Eröffnung der Ausstellung

5⁰⁰ Referate zur Ausstellung

Die Bedeutung der künstlerischen
Betätigung als Heilmittel
Dr. med. G. Bockholt
Dr. med. G. Stavenhagen
Hermann Kirchner

pünktlich 6³⁰ Dr. med. K. König
**Krankheiten unserer Zeit
in ihrer geistigen Gestalt**

pünktlich 8³⁰ Dr. med. G. Suchantke
**Ist der Krebs eine heilbare
Zeitkrankheit?**

Dienstag, den 29. November

4⁰⁰ Ausstellung

5⁰⁰ Dr. R. Hauschka
Referat zur Ausstellung:
Zeitgemäße Ernährung

pünktlich 6³⁰ Dr. med. K. König
**Krankheit und Selbst-
erkenntnis**

pünktlich 8³⁰ Dr. W. J. Stein
Das Problem des Todes

Die Ausstellung zeigt wissenschaftliche Versuche
über Fragen der Ernährung und verschiedene
Diätformen. Ferner wird an Hand von Malereien
und Plastiken auf neue Wege einer künstlerischen
Therapie hingewiesen.

Emil Bock with Karl König at the Eisenach conference, Whitsun 1932

Opposite: Programme of a conference in Berlin in 1932

completely out of the ideas of threefolding. In his contribution 'About the Significance of an Independent College for Social Work' König describes the aims and aspirations of this College in terms of 'freedom of teaching and the freedom to act in accordance with individual judgment,' ending his powerful plea with the words:

> This is how I imagine the work of an independent college for social work: that it shall become the ground on which the spiritual image of the human being as needed by the carer, can be taught; but that it should

also become the place from which those people who, in the midst of the spiritual desolation, can stand on their own foundation as carers, can be sent out into the world. It must be possible for this work to be carried out in complete freedom, without any dependence on the state, relying entirely on donations ... As small as this beginning is, it may be able to convey much blessing. Everything arises from a germ which, if cared for in the proper way, may yield good fruit.[17]

Although his initiative was soon to be overtaken by political developments, it was not completely suffocated. König knew that the events of the times could ultimately only be turned in a positive direction through spiritual strength and the development of social structures on the basis of the free human spirit. One may ask whether these words are only applicable to that time or whether they are still valid today, since the problem — however differently it may manifest in the meantime — has still not really been solved.

Karl König took the seed of this endeavour with him and tried to implant it where human souls were ready to receive it. At least until 1936 he managed to continue working in this 'heart of Central Europe,' between Prague, Eisenach and Breslau (now Wroclaw), until embarking on the first leg of his escape and subsequent exile. That this motif should recur later is by no means incidental. We remember the words he wrote in his London solitude: 'Could we not take up a part of Europe's true destiny and transform it into a seed ...?' and then, during the Camphill time at the end of his life: 'A comprehensive curative education is like the developing seed inside a rotting fruit.'[18]

In his farewell letter he describes very clearly — apart from many positive experiences in Pilgramshain — his disappointment at the fact that Ita Wegman's hope for curative education as representing a prototype for community building within the medical-therapeutic movement, had not been taken seriously enough:

> Painful are the more 'internal' experiences: a repeated
> failure of community at the institute and between
> institutes ... and the often blinkered view of the
> outside world in our ranks. And now the loss of
> everything that, until a few months ago, was the
> core of my life.[19]

It is a remarkable fact that after the National Socialist takeover
in Vienna in 1938 and even during his escape, König took the
time to make detailed applications for his new project. He sub-
mitted them to countries that represented potential destinations
for the emigration of the group of former patients and young
students to whom he had been connected there. After it became
clear that France was no longer an option, he applied to Ireland
and Cyprus. In his applications he attempts to clearly formulate
community aims in the mould of the threefold social order, even
including their statutes. The application to Ireland is preserved in
the Archive and contains two appendices that serve as examples
of the intended social structure. The following is an extract from
this application:

> Only the active co-worker is to participate in determining
> the work. Each co-worker needs to have spiritual
> autonomy. He is to work in his own professional field
> without interference and according to his own free
> resolve. Should this work transgress the framework of
> the community, the staff meeting is to bring this fact
> to his attention and encourage him to fit in with the
> community or to resign ... The co-workers need to
> develop an inner striving that enables them to meet the
> challenge of their task every day and every hour ... So the
> meaning of the whole enterprise can only be to serve the
> striving human being, enabling him or her to become an
> ever-stronger Christian, in sacrifice and devotion, as a
> healer receiving the gift of grace.[20]

The document closes with the following remark: 'Such an institution would be unique today and would be a credit to the country in which it would be developed.'[21]

Striving for the reality of threefold social life

After his arrival in Scotland and the beginning of the work there, any 'visible' concern for the threefold social order became completely submerged in the inner work and creating the practical foundations, perhaps comparable to a seed that initially has to disappear into the darkness of the earth. In his personal essays and notebooks occasional traces of this can be found, such as in the essay of the 1940s (reproduced in the appendix) in which he refers to social threefoldness in order to clarify in his own mind the place of the Christian Community within the Camphill movement.

The topic was not intended to be laid aside, but rather to infuse practical life. König adopted the very same starting point from which Rudolf Steiner derived the Threefold Social Order, and attempted through numerous descriptions to make it comprehensible: namely from the threefoldness of the human being itself. In countless lectures, essays and courses Karl König tried to point out this bodily foundation — even including a lecture (of which unfortunately only preparatory notes have been preserved) about the threefold preparation of food through boiling, frying and baking!

Ideally these insights should be take up with the striving heart in order to enable them to flow into daily life, into therapeutic work, and also, especially, into social structures through the commitment to a process of healing transformation. König does not ignore the unresolved social problems that have at best been masked by post-war prosperity. Many lectures — particularly and increasingly in German cities — bear witness to this fact. His admonishing essays, such as 'Does Prosperity make us ill?'

appeared in several journals.[22] The true significance of curative education for social development in general comes more and more to the fore.[23] The courses he gave for members of the 'village communities' also bear special witness to his hopes for the healing influence of this transformative 'social experiment.' The last of these lectures — also held in 1964 — ends with the words, which can be experienced as a legacy.

> Then the social experiment of the village impulse, this little seed of the threefold social order, may gradually grow and spread healing into the illness of our time.[24]

A fundamental break occurred at the beginning of the sixties after König's first health crisis: the building of the first festival hall of the Camphill community. The lectures included here enable us to fully appreciate this building and the significance attached to it. As a building it was intended to manifest threefoldness, which was to have a radiating effect into the community-building processes of Camphill (and potentially further afield), similar to what Rudolf Steiner had intended for the First Goetheanum — in the sense of architecture supporting social forms.

At the same time König initiated an intensive meditative study of the First Goetheanum, the Foundation Stone Meditation and the motifs of the glass windows throughout the whole Camphill movement, by now already active in seven countries. The full history of this 'social building' goes beyond the task of this book, and would need a separate approach to follow up those intentions of social art and community building. In the context of this volume it must suffice to point to the inauguration of Camphill Hall as opening up a new epoch in König's life and activity.

In retrospect it would appear that the construction of this building, for which he had longed so fervently, was instrumental in taking König, by now having renewed his strength, back from exile to Central Europe.

König was only able to make a *beginning* with this new epoch in his life, clearly indicating the germinal nature of this endeavour

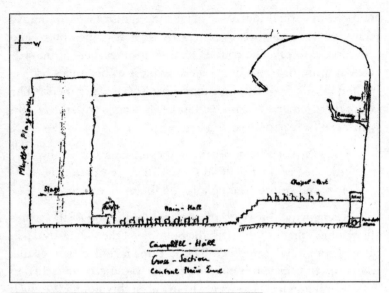

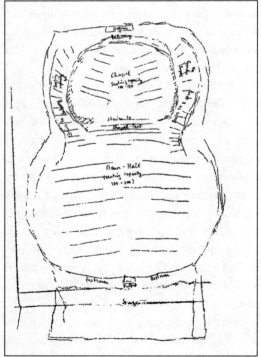

*Sketch section
and plan of
Camphill Hall*

by giving the hall three names at its internal opening. Firstly, Camphill Hall, linking in to the three 'leading stars' of Camphill — Amos Comenius, Count Ludwig Zinzendorf and Robert Owen — the three realms of social life were to be nurtured from here.[25] The second name evokes inner forces, those of memory and conscience, the Hall of Memory and Conscience. The third name makes a connection to the virtue of sacrifice inherent in Irish-Scottish Christianity, that makes development possible. He referred to the name of Iphigenia in connection with this power. Two days later, speaking spontaneously at the official festive opening, to everyone's surprise, instead of the three names already given, he now only mentions the name of Kaspar Hauser.[26]

From an outer point of view it was the increasing number of requests from Germany which took Karl König back to Central Europe, but reading the relevant lectures, it becomes clear that it was an inner calling, probably experienced before or during his journey to Prague and his re-encounter with Karlstejn Castle; a calling that he was only able to take up in a germinal way. Today, almost half a century after Karl König passed into the spiritual world, we can still experience the mood of rebirth, the strength of intention so evident particularly in the Michaelmas lectures. Re-reading these lectures today, when much of anthroposophical work — particularly in the field of curative education — has become strongly institutionalized, a question may arise in us. Is it be possible to pick up those seeds again? Is there a new openness to make the human being the starting point, at a time when confidence in the personal judgment of the individual has long ceased to be the bedrock of professional life? Do we have the courage necessary for this difficult task: to realize that *becoming a human being is truly our social task.*

Wahrheit, Schönheit & Güte,
Das ist der Mensch.

Wahrheit ist der Ausdruck dafür,
daß die ewigen Ideen der Welt ihren
rechten Ausdruck im Denken der Menschen finden.
Wahr ist ein Gedanke, der übereinstimmt
mit dem Wesensinhalt der Idee.

Schönheit offenbart sich dort, wo die
ewigen Ideen mit den Formen, Farben,
Tönen & Worten in Harmonie sind. Wo das
Kleid für die Ideen so adaequat ist, daß man
die Idee in der Wirklichkeit erlebt.

Güte ist dort vorhanden, wo der Geistgehalt
der Idee die Form zu zerschmelzen beginnt;
wo die Form sich ergibt dem Wesen & daraus
die Tat sich gebiert.

Das dreifache Spiel zwischen der Idee
& dem von der Idee erschaffenen Werk,
Das ist Wahrheit, Schönheit & Güte.
Das ist der Mensch
          im Haupt, in der Brust, im Gliedmaßen
Dasein.

Truth, beauty and goodness
This is man
Truth is an expression of the fact
That the eternal ideas of the world
Find their rightful expression in human thinking.
A thought is true if it accords
With the essential content of the idea.

Beauty reveals itself where the
Eternal ideas are in harmony with the forms, colours,
Sounds and words. Where the
Garment for the idea is so adequate that one
Experiences the idea in the reality.

Goodness is present where the spiritual essence
Of the idea begins to melt the form,
Where the form yields itself up to being and out of that
The deed is born.

The threefold interplay between the idea
And the work created by the idea,
This is truth, beauty and goodness.
This is man
In the head, in the chest, in his limb existence.

A verse by Karl König from around 1940

The Threefold
Social Order

Five Lectures

Föhrenbühl and Brachenreuthe, Germany, Easter 1964

The Historical Context of the Threefold Social Order
and the Disintegration of Europe

First Lecture
Föhrenbühl, Monday, March 2, 1964

Dear friends,

Today I shall give an introduction that will provide the historical context in which Rudolf Steiner developed the threefold social order. Without that, it will not be easy to gain a true understanding of this idea of the social organism in a threefold form.

This idea developed during the First World War. The first ideas on this subject came to Rudolf Steiner in 1916, and in 1917 and 1918 he endeavoured to formulate these ideas in such a way that they could be written as short memoranda. These memoranda were presented to leading personalities at the time, including the Crown Prince of Baden who became Chancellor of the German Empire in the last year of the war, Foreign Minister Kühlmann, and the Austrian Emperor. This did hardly any good and we have to admit that, outwardly speaking, the whole endeavour to promote the threefolding of the social organism had no effect whatsoever. The movement failed. We must openly admit this, and it would be falsifying history to claim that

Rudolf Steiner had any kind of outer success with it. Through their lack of understanding, his followers, our anthroposophical friends, were unable to represent these ideas in such a way that they could be truly understood. This is not intended as a reproach, for none of us would have been capable of it. Although the trends of the time were actually calling for such a threefolding, nevertheless it did not to become reality.

This meant that from 1920/21 onwards the idea of the threefold social order had to be gradually buried, and Rudolf Steiner suffered enormously through things turning out that way. Nevertheless, the fact remains that this idea of the threefold social order is intimately bound up with the second decade of the twentieth century in which it was born. It is also not without good reason that we are occupying ourselves with it today. This year exactly half a century will have passed since the outbreak of the First World War, this world war, through which in effect those social structures that had become established in Europe and America since the beginning of the modern era, were dissolved and broken. The First World War was one of the most powerful historical events in the entire development of mankind. We are not yet able to fully appreciate this, as we are only half a century away from it, as our lives are still immersed in its aftereffects. But through this First World War, the social structures which had evolved since the fourteenth, fifteenth, sixteenth centuries perished.

What kind of social structure was this? This was the first attempt at establishing a social and political structure in the fifth post-Atlantean epoch, that is, the first European attempt to structure state organisms in such a way as to create the possibility for the freedom of the individual and the individual personality to unfold. Only from a superficial point of view would we be able to say, looking back at ancient Rome and the decay of the great Roman Empire, or looking back at the decline of the great Egyptian or Persian empires (and we could go further and further back), that similar processes happened here. This is, however, not the case. What is happening around us today is something new; historically it is something so utterly new that we can hardly find anything to compare it with, unless we were to adopt a completely superficial point of view. Several present-day historians have gradually come to recognize this fact. If any of you have time to study a work such as *Freedom and Domination* by the recently deceased Rüstow,* you will discover that here is a man who has woken up to the realization that our age cannot be regarded merely as a repetition of many previous epochs, but that our epoch represents something essentially new. This coming into being of the new has been severely shaken by the chaos of the First World War, and through the events that followed and led to the Second World War, it has been completely destroyed. This is why today we stand amid the ruins of social structures, from which, stone by stone, the house of future social structures will have to be built up anew. The social renewal that Rudolf Steiner had attempted to bring about did in fact not succeed in the twenties.

But now we must ask ourselves what really happened in the time since the fifteenth, sixteenth, seventeenth centuries. What was the real nature of the social and political order that evolved? The evolution of the modern age can be described in various ways. It is for example possible to state that this modern age is in reality nothing but the beginning of the kind of thinking characteristic of natural science. The great Galileo (whose four-hundredth birthday was two weeks ago), and the great scientific thinkers of the sixteenth and seventeenth centuries such as Copernicus and Kepler, initiated the revolution in human thinking, where an understanding of nature is based on experience and experiment. That is one aspect.

However, one could also say that the modern era — and here

---

* Alexander Rüstow (1885–1963) was an economist and sociologist who in 1918 was involved in the November Revolution in Germany and in the resistance movement during the Third Reich. He was one of the men who shaped the West German economy after the Second World War.

I mean everything encompassed by the recent centuries — is characterized by the fact that the Reformation, the religious Reformation spread further and further afield. The Reformation really endeavours to overcome the old religious forms, the traditional forms of the Christian faith, by referring back to the individual human personality, endeavouring to regulate his personal relationship to the supersensible world or to God. This too is a fully justified characterization of the inception of the modern era. Thus on the one hand we have the development of scientific thinking, taking as its reference point sensory experience, experiment and observation, and on the other hand, the Reformation.

A further significant component are the voyages of exploration — the fact that from Europe, from England, Holland, Portugal, Spain — seafarers set out to experience the roundness of the earth, to unlock distant continents, to widen what until then had been physically narrow. People broke out of their medieval towns and dwellings; they wanted to know what really existed in north and south, in east and west. People had known all this before, but now they wanted to experience it with their senses; they wanted to carry out the experiment of the discovery of unknown lands, and this they did. This too is a characteristic of the dawning of the modern era.

And finally something took place, a process we still find ourselves in today, and that is the mechanization of existence: the emergence of mechanics, of technology, the organization of practical and industrial life, of cultural life in the light of the magnificent discoveries which were made. This has, of course, transformed the life of nations, the organization of state institutions.

And what has all this actually led to? Dear friends, the thing that actually arose from this is what we would call the centralized state. In the twelfth or ninth centuries there was no such thing as a centralized state. Only since the beginning of the modern age has it been possible for the centralized state to develop. What do we mean by a centralized state? It is a concept used in political science. By 'centralized state' we mean a political structure that encompasses and governs most areas of social life.

All this arose from what I described earlier. The moment discoveries of new territories had been made, these newly discovered territories and continents were not left alone, nor *could* they be left alone, but what happened was that Spain, Portugal, England, Holland and finally — lagging behind as usual — Germany too became colonial powers. This means that streams of people went forth from these countries to the newly discovered continents and settled there as Spaniards, Portuguese, Englishmen, Germans, Dutchmen, and these territories — which in fact became regions of exploitation — were annexed by these various states, with the result that England became an empire, Spain became a short-lived empire, Holland became an empire. The immediate effect was that the exploitation of the economic process was annexed by the state. The state became not only the protector but also the beneficiary of those economic markets that arose in South Africa, in America, or wherever. India became part of Great Britain, Indo-China a part of France and Indonesia a part of Holland. The state became the bearer of the economy.

At the same time another thing arose, of which we are hardly aware any longer today, something which even twenty or thirty years ago was still an essential part of the life of the state: the development of a state church. Churches became part of the state. Religious life became part of the state; this arose through the Reformation. Regardless of how the Reformation came about — whether from a ruler in England under Henry VIII, or from a priest as in Germany with Luther, the fact that Reformation took place at all and that the individual person was to find his own relationship to the supersensible world — this became politicized and became subject to the state. For example in the sixteenth and seventeenth centuries the principle of *cuius regio, eius religio* held sway, which meant that the individual had to embrace the religion of his ruler. So if I had lived in Saxony

I would have had to be Protestant, and if I had lived in Austria I would have had to be Catholic, or I would have been forced to move. This is a development that was not only confined to the dark period of the Thirty Years War but has shown itself in different ways ever since.

There is something else which needs to be considered. Religious life became a concern of the state; the economic life was regulated by the state, while the state itself was determined by the element of Roman law inherent in it. This was the legacy of the fourth post-Atlantean epoch, and the centralized state was the social organization through which the different spheres of human life were mixed together, united and forged into a single unit. Within this structure it was quite possible for people to pursue their own destinies. This structure can be regarded as perfectly justified up to a certain moment. This moment occurred around the turn of the seventeenth and eighteenth centuries. It was the time of the Industrial Revolution, the French Revolution and the Napoleonic Wars. This was a nodal point in history of comparable significance to that of the First World War in our century. From that time onwards the centralized state could only be upheld by political power.

I don't want to go into the historical details of this at the moment, but one thing ought to be mentioned. Through the Industrial Revolution something dreadful and yet necessary entered human thinking and activity. With the mass production of goods people stopped producing only as many shoes as there were feet to wear them; suddenly the idea was spread that we must make progress and that goods must be made more cheaply; all people and more should be able to wear shoes, all should have armchairs and tables, all should have clothes, everyone should not only have two or three suits but twenty suits, and so forth. This became possible because through technical innovation these goods could be produced in bulk.

This had a further consequence that needs to be clearly understood. What happened was that suddenly labour was no longer simply labour, but labour — to use a Marxist phrase — had become a commodity. People were able to sell their labour. The activity of the muscles, the will to work, was sold. It was sold to those who, through their capital, had the possibility to set up so many machines that they were able to degrade the proletariat to the level of slave labour. We should never forget that the darkest time in this respect was the middle of the nineteenth century; children had to work in factories from the age of five, parents were forced, or experienced the necessity, to have a dozen children so that they could send them into the factories as quickly as possible, so the few pennies that these children took home for a working day of between 12 and 14 hours, could buy food and drink. Not until towards the end of the nineteenth century, were laws enforced that regulated child labour in England, Germany, Scotland, Holland. The nineteenth century was indeed the century in which labour was degraded to the level of a commodity.

Related to this something else took place that had a similarly devastating effect on social life: capital embraced the ownership of land. People came to believe, and still believe today, that the best investment was in land. This meant that agriculture was undermined and itself became a slave to capital. This meant — and these two things are closely connected — that human labour was degraded to the level of a commodity, and that land, part of Mother Earth, became an investment. All this was decisive for the social life of the nineteenth century. These things provided the foundation for centralized states.

We shall return to this in the next lecture. Here I will merely point out that an insanity such as National Socialism was only able to gain a foothold in Germany through the fact that two things came together, leading to the most shameful actions of the century: the industrial barons of the Ruhr, having degraded labour to the level of a commodity, allied themselves to the powerful landowners in Prussia, in the east of this country, thus preparing the horse on which barbarism could invade Central Europe.

This needs to be said, no matter how many or how few are prepared to hear it. This was the result of what had been prepared in the nineteenth century. The fact that land became an investment and that labour was degraded to the level of a commodity, this has to be stamped out. Some of those here now may recollect the sound of the first warning bugle-call when in the spring of 1912 the *Titanic* sank, taking with her representatives of those levels of society which had brought about the situation I have just characterized. This clarion-call was scarcely heeded. And then came June 28, 1914. I still remember that day as though it were yesterday: it was a day of bright sunshine, a Sunday; the people around Vienna were out in the open air; I was by the Danube with my father, and suddenly it seemed as though life had come to a standstill, and though I could not understand it, I had a kind of premonition. The news came that Archduke Franz Ferdinand had been assassinated in Sarajevo. We know what was expressed a month later by Sir Edward Grey, the British Foreign Minister, on August 1: 'The lamps are going out all over Europe: we shall not see them lit again in our lifetime.'[1] Since then the lights over Europe have not come back on, they have remained off. In that First World War twelve million people were killed and thirty million crippled. Mankind endured all this, then went into the Second World War and is rapidly sliding towards a third.

In 1918 came the disastrous Treaty of Versailles. Through the ruling circles — today it can be said, through the misguided politicians at the time — Clémenceau, Lloyd George and Woodrow Wilson, the possibility of a renewal of Europe was arbitrarily scuppered through stupidity and an autocratic mindset. Clémenceau was the 'father' of de Gaulle. The madness taking place in France today has its precursors in Poincaré and Clémenceau. What is happening in Great Britain at present is very similar to Lloyd George's misdeeds. And what were Woodrow Wilson's intentions? He wanted *one* thing: somehow he had realized that the centralized state was finished and that something else had to take its place. And — without either realizing or intending it — he took up the Napoleonic idea of the nation state. This was the worst thing imaginable, that nationalities should join together to form states!

Wilson was very sincere about this, but the others deceived him both openly and behind his back. At Versailles Clémenceau and Lloyd George, wanting to forestall a unification of the Germans of Austria and the Germans of Central Europe, led Wilson to believe that they were going to conclude a treaty with Austria in order to protect that country's freedom in relation to Germany. This was something Woodrow Wilson could understand. In a similar way they deceived him, to put it bluntly, wherever they could with regard to any number of other treaties. Of course Clémenceau and Lloyd George realized that states were all well and good, but if taken seriously France and Britain would lose power, would lose their colonies, and thus their sphere of influence. So they concluded treaties in the most underhand and deceitful manner in order to prevent other national states from actually coming into being. Nevertheless some states were formed, such as Poland, Yugoslavia, Czechoslovakia and Hungary. What had once been Austria was torn apart and destroyed. What could truly have become Central Europe was crushed.

However, another factor was added to the equation. Amid this chaos the consciousness of the proletariat began to awake, and with the awakening of the proletariat a longing for social reform began to dawn. It was believed that this reform could be channelled by offering the workers a cultural life that was materialistic and agnostic. They responded to this, and we can see the results today. The workers have turned into a class of well-to-do, satisfied *petite bourgeoisie* who sometimes still talk about the proletarian revolution, while the word itself has become a completely empty phrase. This will be a theme of the next lecture.

This was the context into which Rudolf Steiner placed his idea of the threefold social order, an idea that takes account of the individual as well as the state in outlining evolutionary social forms appropriate for our time. Rudolf Steiner completely rejected the national state. Equally he rejected the centralized state; he rejected both what was coming from the past, as well as what was being advocated out of a deceptive view of the future. Between these two he now placed something that can be described in the following way.

The state needs to be confined to those aspects of social life that constitute the life of rights. Its proper task is to regulate the legal inter-relationships of its citizens, and it must not interfere either in the economic life or with cultural life. The state is the organization through which the citizen is legally held in his proper place. In the next few centuries things will unfold in such a way that we will be able to say to ourselves: the citizen enjoys the legal protection of the state. The judiciary, the police, all this belongs to the realm of the state.

Everything that constitutes the economy, as well as everything that constitutes labour and landed property, will be separated from the state. Economy is nothing but the production, sale and distribution of goods. This production of goods can be brought about through agriculture, through industrial production or by any other means. But the production, distribution and sale of goods constitutes a realm which does not belong to the sphere of the state; it is a realm which should be administered independently of the state in an associative way by those producing, distributing and selling goods. However, labour, the legal aspect of labour belongs to the state, since labour is not a commodity. We will come back to this issue. Land too does not belong to the economic sphere. However, property law, just as labour law, is part of the state. But the goods themselves and what is required for the production of goods, for their distribution and sale, that constitutes the economic life.

Then there is the sphere of the free, independent spiritual-cultural life. This is the realm of education, of religion, of research, of art. All this, as well as capital, belongs to this sphere. Capital is part of the sphere of the free spiritual life, as capital is only justified where it is a question of the realization of impulses of free spiritual life. Capital is not owned, but constitutes the means of realization of free spiritual life.

You see, in this way a threefold structure comes into being instead of a centralized one. Parts of this are gradually coming about, albeit amid epileptic fits, for example in an organization such as the European Common Market,* where there is an endeavour to develop associations within the economic sphere. But immediately, along comes someone as misguided as de Gaulle, who wants to turn it into a political organization, and of course everybody falls for this and now wants to create a homogenized political Europe. We need to be awake to these things. In my opinion the heap of ruins on which we are standing today nevertheless shows certain growing points of social renewal. The only problem is that people nowadays are barely capable of perceiving them, and as a result they are bound to perish time and again.

---

* The Common Market was founded by the Treaty of Rome in 1957 as predecessor of the European Community, which later became the European Union.

The Failure of
New Social Endeavours
Meditative Images for a
Deeper Understanding of the
Principle of Threefolding

Second Lecture
Brachenreuthe, Sunday, March 8, 1964

Dear friends,

Today we shall continue with what we started last time. We began by sketching the historical background of the events which, at the end of the First World War and at the beginning of the twenties, led Rudolf Steiner to put the idea of the threefold structure of the social organism into the world, speaking about it in front of thousands of people. We also faced the fact that this initial endeavour was a complete failure. The idea of threefolding was understood by only very few people. The idea was either ridiculed or rejected by leading personalities of the time. As a result, further developments followed which I shall try to characterize now. Our aim will be to create a kind of backcloth for the development of present-day social institutions and endeavours.

Last time we focussed on developing a historical understanding of centralized states, namely those European and later also American institutions through which the state came to be the carrier of what was really a threefold social organism: the economic life, the legal/rights sphere and the cultural life. The fact that these three spheres exist needs no explanation; it is obvious; it is an unshakeable reality. Otherwise we might as well ask whether we have ears, eyes and limbs. It requires no proof. In the same way the existence of the three spheres of the social life requires no proof; they are simply the constituent parts of the human social organism.

In the centralized state — which to a large extent still exists today — these three spheres have become intertwined. The European centralized state began to direct economic life, to rule out of the life of rights and profoundly to influence cultural life. We have already spoken about this. But something else has arisen, particularly in our century, through the unfortunate policy of Woodrow Wilson on the one hand and through the misguided policies that followed at the end of the Second World War: the emergence of nation states. Everything we encounter nowadays by way of cultural life, political life, economic life is the catastrophic consequence of the gradual emergence of nation states.

Colonialism failed to educate those people who for centuries were exploited and dominated by centralized states (which are themselves ruled by economics). Instead, these totally exploited and uneducated people were granted independence only after having been infused with the poison of nationalism. This in turn has led to the continual eruptions and will lead to further eruptions that destroy the entire political life of the world. It is surprising that out of a completely misguided idealism people nowadays applaud when a country such as Congo or Nigeria, or any other such state, is given what is called 'independence.' The responsibility for this does not rest with these states but only with those who, over the last three or four centuries, have failed to see and understand what is the rightful due of these native peoples and to act accordingly.

This means that we have two things here — and we have to see this clearly if we are to avoid simply mechanically repeating the ideas of threefolding or mindlessly perpetuating any old newspaper gossip by which we are continuously misled today. On the one hand we have the endeavour to proclaim centralized states and on the other hand the endeavour to proclaim nation states. We saw that the centralized states have their origins in the Anglo-Saxon countries, where in the last few centuries the centralized state was developed in such a way that the economic life became the determining influence, forcing the rights life and the cultural life more and more under its dominion. This can still be experienced quite clearly today in England, Scotland, in America, in Holland, Scandinavia, etc. Everything under the Anglo-Saxon influence wishes to cling to the old utopia of the centralized state under the control of the economic life.

Where is the origin of the nation states to be found? Just as the centralized state had its origins in the Anglo-Saxon realm, the nation state had its origin in one particular region of Europe, and that is France. As early as the fourteenth century, in the reign of Philip the Fair, who enticed the Pope to Avignon and held him prisoner there, and who crushed the great international organization of the Knights Templar, the idea of nationalism arose. This idea of nationalism then developed further under various subsequent rulers of France — I cannot go into the details of French history now, but if you were really to study the phenomena, you would find that it is nothing but an emergent nation state — and reached a certain flowering during the reign of Louis XIV. And then Napoleon endeavoured to transform the whole of Europe into nation states. Napoleon wanted to break up Europe into many diverse nation states, installing his generals or relatives as rulers over each one. It was nothing but an 'old boys' network' designed to destroy Europe and to achieve the complete domination of

61

the idea of French nationalism. What we are experiencing today under Monsieur de Gaulle is nothing but a renewed attempt to set the idea of national France to shine over the whole earth as the 'sun of all people.' I beg you to take this fact on board. This is nothing but the latest attempt, albeit bordering on the ridiculous, at establishing French nationalism.

It is important to look at what has arisen in the last few centuries on the one hand from England and on the other from France. Joan of Arc had the task of driving the English out of France, to end the Hundred Years War by confining England to its islands and to make available to France its own continental domain. In England this led to the development of the centralized state in conjunction with colonialism and the expansion of the entire economic life. On the other hand the idea of the nation state was connected with France. These two developmental trends *had* to arise; they were necessary. This happened simultaneously with the dawning of the age of the consciousness soul at the beginning of the fifteenth century. Here I see two entirely different, yet necessary, trends for the social configuration of states emerging from England and France. These permeated Europe, and at the end of the nineteenth and the beginning of the twentieth centuries something new arose which, by means of revolutions, tried to permeate the elements of the centralized as well as the nation state. This was something new, something completely unexpected for those who were simply living their carefree existence. Now suddenly a migration of people began in Europe, not a horizontal but a vertical migration, in such a way that what had been the lower classes of society started pressing upwards; those who until then had been servants, serfs, labourers, agricultural workers now started to migrate to the towns and cities and became the industrial proletariat. This took place first and foremost in England, and this led to what is called the Industrial Revolution. This is where the first cotton processing machines, the spinning machines were invented, giving rise to the first industrial economy.

In France, however, this process took a different form. Here the poor, the oppressed, the servants, the agricultural labourers rebelled against their masters, against the upper classes. This was a completely different revolution from the Industrial Revolution that took place in England. It would be quite wrong to equate the one with the other and simply say: well, it took place here in one way and there in another. The Industrial Revolution took place in the economic life. The French Revolution, on the other hand, in which for the first time a slogan such as *liberty, equality, fraternity* was employed, did not take place in the economic life but solely within the rights sphere. We must be clear about this if we are to be able to do justice to both these revolutions.

At the same time, in Central Europe — Germany as a socio-political entity did not yet exist at that time — quite a different revolution took place, a kind of renaissance and renewal in cultural life. Poetry and philosophy suddenly took on a completely new life. In England there was a revolution within economic life, in France a revolution in the rights sphere, while in the German regions of Central Europe a revolution within the spiritual-cultural life took place. These were three interconnected processes, albeit completely different within themselves and from each other. In England the masses were concerned with a demand for fraternity, in France they wanted equality and in Germany they demanded freedom. I am describing all this because it forms the historical background for everything that emerges at the beginning of the twentieth century as the idea of the threefold structure of the social organism. Thus we are dealing here with historical events that were a preparation for what was to emerge a hundred years later.

These three starting points at the turn of the eighteenth to the nineteenth centuries were later wiped out again. In England growing colonialism swept along the Industrial Revolution as if to say: there, have a little share of what we who are exploiting colonies are earning! The French Revolution was destroyed by

Napoleonism, which was a form of nationalism, and in Germany all striving for freedom was swallowed up by the charming Biedermeier (bourgeois) lifestyle in the mid-nineteenth century, making way for completely new conditions, which no longer had anything to do with liberty, equality and fraternity. Yet that migration of people which broke through vertically from below was unstoppable — despite Biedermeier, despite colonialism and despite Napoleon's nationalism. Something started to emerge which the leading circles could not comprehend at all, but which now began to stretch and strain more and more like an awakening giant.

What was it that emerged? Those who have not lived through the events at the beginning of the century and did not experience what social revolution was and what it signified at the time, are unable to really grasp what it meant when the workers rose up in their hundreds of thousands, that they demanded their rights, that a common will suddenly began to spread internationally, overcoming all national boundaries. The ideals that lived in those people at that time, albeit somewhat lacking in definition, were a kind of springtime hope for new social conditions. Anyone who had marched in those ranks himself knows what was alive deeply unconsciously in those people at the time. We no longer come across this nowadays, when a certain apathy is a characteristic feature of the present generation, and in any case there is no longer any need for it. The labour movement has been conquered by degrading the workers to the level of *petite bourgeoisie;* owing to the fact that most of them own a smaller or a bigger car, they no longer experience the need to transform social life.

But men like Robert Owen, like Lassalle, Marx, Engels and others experienced that the formation of a new social order had become necessary due to the demise of liberalism in the middle of the nineteenth century and the failure of the middle classes, who had become inert. But the very moment this realization

64

began to dawn, when this giant of a vertical revolution began to flex its muscles, certain things took place, which one needs to be conscious of when one studies history. On the one hand the idea of evolution was hijacked by Darwinism; the great and powerful idea of evolution, which dawned in the minds of thinkers such as Herder and Goethe, Karl Ernst von Baer and others as a new world conception, was suddenly reduced to a 'struggle for existence.'

At the same time something else happened. For what was it that actually happened during the Industrial Revolution? The Industrial Revolution spawned collective labour, which began not in twos and threes and tens, but in hundreds and thousands. For the first time a kind of collective arose in the economic life that had not been seen since Egyptian times. This labour collective was hijacked by capitalism just as the idea of evolution had been appropriated by Darwinism. What in Darwinism was mere theory was put into practical effect through capitalism. Capitalism made the struggle for existence a reality, and what could the workers and their prophets do, but take up the war cry themselves and coin the devastating phrase 'class war.' Suddenly there were two opposing camps: capitalists and proletarians. Instead of freedom, equality and brotherhood, there was class war. This essentially marked the end of the nation state as well as the centralized state. There was no way out, and therefore the First World War broke out. That war effectively wiped out all previously existing social structures, and at the end of that First World War, the idea of the threefold structure of the social organism was born. But instead of taking up this idea people clung to old thought forms and outdated emotions. They persisted with their old mistakes and then proceeded to establish national central-ized states, or, if you will, centralized national states. That is the history, the social history, of the period between the two world wars, between 1918 and 1939.

What I am about to say may be difficult to grasp. Through

the influence of the West, starting from England and to some extent also from America, Bolshevism developed in Russia: the idea of the centralized state came about in the East, in Russia, in an exaggerated form. The idea of National Socialism and Fascism, originating in France, also manifested in an exaggerated form elsewhere. In this way two centralized nation states arose. This inevitably led to the total corruption of all social conditions and as a result the Second World War became inevitable. It could not have been otherwise because these developments did not represent social solutions but social insanity.

In a sense the Second World War is still continuing today. In fact we are living in the middle of a war, although we have enough to eat, although we can build houses. We are living in the Cold War, and the terrible thing is that this cold war is the only way of preventing the hot war that is continually knocking at the door. We cannot still speak of a social order today. Such a thing no longer exists. What we have are interim social arrangements, and everyone knows that it is questionable whether they will still be functioning in six months. The mere existence of states today is a utopian concept. Of course there are national states in Africa, but do you believe that the German Republic, whether in the West or in the East, is a state, or that England or France are states? They are parts of power blocks that no longer know how they should behave towards each other, and underneath all that — I am describing it in such a way as to make visible the essence of the matter — seeds of the idea of threefoldness are emerging in the most diverse places. Like a rare magic herb, it appears now in one place and then in another, trying to break through here and there. Time and again it is crushed, and yet it persists.

The question remains as to how the idea of threefoldness actually came about. Where does it come from? Did Rudolf Steiner simply suddenly discover it and then, having been aware of it for thirty years, write it down in 1916 in a subsidiary chapter of his book *Riddles of the Soul?* Or had this idea tried to come to expression much earlier, somewhere, at some time?

One thing can be stated with confidence. Just as the tremendous idea of the evolution of organisms awoke in mankind at the turn of the eighteenth to the nineteenth centuries — particularly in Herder, but then also in Geoffroy Saint-Hilaire, and Lamarck,* in Goethe and in others, a concept that could hardly have been foreseen and had never before been suspected or known about — in the same way did the idea of threefoldness arise as something quite new at the turn of the eighteenth to the nineteenth centuries. While Rudolf Steiner was the first one really to have brought all this into a synthesis, it had nevertheless broken through every now and again in previous centuries. In the fifteenth and sixteenth centuries, for example, the alchemists and Rosicrucians spoke about the fact that there is a threefold process in nature: *sal, mercury* and *sulfur.* By this they did not mean the substances of salt, mercury and sulphur, but the *processes.* The *sal* process signified the salt process and the structure-forming process, *mercury* the balancing process, *sulfur* the process of burning and combustion. This first seed of the idea of threefoldness was then picked up for example by Paracelsus, who introduced it into the realm of medicine, not only into the preparation of remedies but also into the realm of pathology.† He spoke of *sal, mercury* and *sulfur* illnesses, describing them according to *sal, mercury* and *sulfur* functions. Here we see something breaking through.

Centuries later a German philosopher and psychologist, who is completely unknown today, refers to the fact that within the human soul three processes take place: Thinking, feeling and will. This man was called Johannes Nikolaus Tetens. If Rudolf

---

* Étienne Geoffroy Saint-Hilaire (1772–1844), zoologist and theologian, worked in Paris together with the natural history researcher Jean-Baptiste Lamarck (1744–1829) on the theory of evolution.

† Theophrastus Bombastus von Hohenheim (1493–1541), also known as Paracelsus, was physician, alchemist, mystic and philosopher.

Steiner had not referred to him, we would know nothing about him today. Thus we have *sal, mercury* and *sulfur* in the processes of nature; thinking, feeling and will in the human soul; then a short time later liberty, equality and fraternity in social life. These are germs of the idea of threefoldness that started to emerge in Europe in previous centuries. It would be wrong to say that Rudolf Steiner picked up on these ideas. Through the fact that Rudolf Steiner had begun to look at the human organism and to describe the phenomena, he was able to give a comprehensive account of the threefold human being. He described it as being made up of three different spheres: a nerve-sense organization, a rhythmic organization and a metabolic-limb organization, not as parts independent of one another, but as members with inter-penetrating functions. He describes the nerve-sense organization as the formative organization that receives impressions passively like a mirror and is concentrated in the head; the metabolic-limb organization as essentially active and transformative and then, creating a balance between above and below, breath and heart-beat in the rhythmic organization.

So here we have the nerve-sense system, the rhythmic system and the metabolic-limb system, and the moment we begin to recognize this fact, we also know that the salt process works in the nerve-sense system, giving form and shape, forming salt, forming bones, that the mercury process works in the rhythmic organization in a balancing way, dissolving and forming, forming and dissolving, and the sulphur process works in the metabolic-limb organization as a process of heat and combustion, a process of 'firing up,' as it were. At the same time we recognize that the nerve-sense organization is the bearer of thinking, the rhythmic organization the bearer of our feeling life and the metabolic-limb system the bearer of our life of will. In this way the idea of threefoldness becomes a key, designed to unlock world secrets.

In our head consciousness we are awake, in our rhythmic system lives dream-consciousness and in our metabolic-limb system we are asleep, as it were. So we have waking, dreaming, sleeping; thinking, feeling, will; *sal, mercury* and *sulfur*.

Thinking — waking consciousness — *sal*
Feeling — dream consciousness — *mercury*
Will — sleep-consciousness — *sulfur*

To be able to experience all this as a synthesis is a prerequisite for gaining any kind of understanding of the idea of the three-folding of the social order. This will not be possible without a renewal of the understanding of the human being that under-lies the idea of threefoldness. A renewal of social life will only emerge gradually from spiritual-cultural life and just not from economic life or the rights sphere.

Now if we look, let us say, at the life of plants and really observe a root, a leaf or a flower, we find that here too there is threefoldness. In the root we will find the salt-formation proc-esses at work; in the leaves, in the interplay between light and shade, between the taking in and the giving off of carbon dioxide and oxygen, there rhythm is at work, breathing, the mercurial element. In the flowers we have the dispersing, the disintegrat-ing element but also the process of fructification. Then we begin to see how the head of the human being corresponds to the root of the plant, and the flower of the plant corresponds to the metabolic system of the human being, and that top, middle and bottom in the plant are not the same as in the human being. The plant grows upwards from the salt-process, enters the mercury process and unfolds upwards towards the flowering process, i.e. towards the metabolism, the sulphur process.

Just as the plant is formed in its threefold structure, we find that the social spheres have a similar configuration. However, the economic sphere is not (as one might assume at first glance) the metabolic-limb system just because this is the sphere of work and nutrition. We can only arrive at a real understand-ing of the economic system when we realize that it is like the root of the plant in that it takes in the given conditions. The soil supplies the farmer with substances, while minerals and metals are extracted from mines. The human being constructs machines for industrial production. The foundations for production are to be found in the ground, and this is where the economic life unfolds. Upwards from there — in a mercurial way — the life of rights develops, and right at the top the flowers and fruits of the spiritual life unfold. This may be a picture; one cannot say, however, that it is *merely* a picture, but actually it is a seed for the understanding of the three spheres of human social life that are still not sufficiently penetrated with understanding.

Now of course we can also add that the human being with his limb- and metabolic system stands within this 'root-head' of the economic system; the human being as an individual as well as the many people doing work together are anchored in the root-head of the economic system. The rhythmic human being breathes within the rights life of his own country and just as the human being works within the economic system, he expresses himself within the rights sphere; this is why we use the expression *to pronounce judgment*. It cannot be otherwise, for only where the same language is spoken, can a uniform system of justice develop. It is nonsense to believe that the law is the same everywhere. The law is just *not* the same. The law develops according to the requirements of the people speaking a common language. What appears as justice to us may be experienced as injustice by others, because, unlike the economic life, justice is not something international. The economy encompasses the whole earth: that is the head. The sphere of rights, of law, belongs to the individual peoples, and in the flower of this plant we can envisage the head of man, engendering creative thought.

In walking, speaking and thinking, we have those capacities which make the human being into a social being. No animal can ever achieve this: in the first three years of life the human learns to walk, which is later transmuted into work, enabling him to participate in the economic life; he learns to speak, which enables

70

him, upon reaching maturity, to have equal rights with his fellow citizens, and through the fact that he learns to think, he is able to share in the freedom of the life of the spirit and of culture. If we can begin to see this, if we take in such pictures and meditate on them imaginatively and imagine them meditatively, then fundamental insights will develop which can become seeds for a future threefolding of the social organism.

The Spiritual Dimension of Human Development
The Higher Senses as a Social Legacy

Third Lecture
Föhrenbühl, Palm Sunday, March 22, 1964

Dear friends,

Tonight we shall attempt to take another step in our contemplation of the threefold nature of both the human and the social organism. In the first two lectures we considered some historical aspects, looking at the centuries that have passed since the inception of the consciousness soul. Within this historical context we looked at the evolution of certain types of state such as the centralized state, the national state, in order to create a certain backdrop for what we might call the proclamation of threefold social life through Rudolf Steiner. Then we tried to explore the actual origins of the idea of threefoldness, the antecedents within cultural life that gradually gave rise to it. This again took us back to the age of the consciousness soul. We saw how an idea such as that of *sal, mercury* and *sulfur* arose within the Rosicrucian alchemical stream of spiritual life; how later certain philosophers were able to describe the threefold nature of human soul life as consisting of thinking, feeling and will, and how within those developments that eventually gave rise to the French Revolution, the three ideals of liberty, fraternity and equality were proclaimed. We saw how a threefold structure was gradually perceived — first in nature, then in the human soul and finally in social relationships — and how eventually, from 1916, the idea of the true threefold nature of the human being as such as well as the threefoldness of the social organism was formulated by Rudolf Steiner.

In fact it can be said that quietly, amid the storms of the First World War, this mighty idea of threefoldness was born: the fact that there is such a thing — which we often refer to casually without having even the first idea of its true significance — as a nerve-sense system, and that this is connected with the formation of concepts and thinking; that we have a rhythmic system, and that this rhythmic system is connected with emotional perception and feeling; that we have a metabolic-limb system, through which the will comes to manifestation. These are really ideas, imaginations, truths that are calling for more than the empty words with which we normally refer to them. The idea of the threefold structure of the social organism came about through Rudolf Steiner, following on from, and in connection with, the idea of the threefold nature of the human being consisting of body, soul and spirit.

What I am about to say may sound uncomfortable. If we are honest with ourselves, and ask ourselves honestly, what do we really imagine when we speak about the economic life or when we speak about the rights sphere and above all, when we speak about a free spiritual life? What do we imagine? If we are completely honest, we have to say: nothing at all. Words, words, which we use to cover over and mask something that cannot yet be contemplated. Please forgive me for being so blunt, and of course what I am saying applies just as much to myself as to everybody else. The only difference is that I *know* that I know nothing; and I would merely like to make you realize that you too know nothing. How can we possibly begin to understand the spiritual life, the rights sphere, the economic life? Our concern here will be to try to understand what it actually means that the human being lives within a society.

Aristotle expressed this fact in rather derogatory way — it never appealed to me — when he states that the human being is a *zoön politikon*, which means, a political beast or animal. That sounds derogatory, but he is right nevertheless. The human being — and that includes each one of us — is only really human because he lives among human beings, with human beings and devotes himself to human beings. Without other human beings we ourselves could not be human beings. We forget this all too easily, particularly if we are anthroposophists and believe that freedom consists in the fact that we exist, but I really only exist by virtue of the fact that I am with others, and that others are with me. I do not mean this in a philosophic sense but in a very real sense. And I feel that if we are to achieve any kind of understanding of the threefold social organism, we have to begin to grasp the fact that man really is a *zoön politikon,* and that it is only through this fact that he *can* be a human being. It is not possible for me to be a human being without other human beings. There are some terrible exceptions to this — solitary confinement in a prison, for example, or insanity, which means being excluded from communication with other human beings. There is also the practice of anchorites (or hermits) which I consider to be just as dreadful because it actually dehumanizes the very person who practises it. It may lead him to God or even make him more God-like, but it cannot humanize him.

The human being can only be truly human together with others. On his own he is not a human being. We are born out of other human beings, fed and taught by other human beings, loved and hated by other human beings. This is the reality of our life, and we must begin to realize it in such a way that we begin to understand that the human being does not merely consist of a physical body, an etheric body, an astral body, an I, of body, soul and spirit; above all we consist of everything constituted by our fellow human beings spread across the earth as the totality of mankind: the people among whom we live, the family we were born into, the karmic group into which we are received between birth and death. It is only the totality of all these relationships that makes a human being. Without it we are not human beings. Developing an inner perception of this reality is the first step on the way to an understanding of what it means to be a human being on earth among other human beings. This is the first thing we have to focus on.

The next thing is to ask: how does it come about, how is it possible for us to be a *zoön politikon?* Animals are not political beasts. Animals can be together in herds; they join together in associations, utilitarian associations. An anthill, a termite mound, these are functional associations. Herds are formed to facilitate propagation and to make life possible. This has nothing to do with community in the sense in which this arises as political or social life among human beings. That is why those compari-sons that are frequently made — like the comparison of an ant colony with a human state, or of a conglomeration of cells with the political state and such like — represent a complete aberra-tion of thinking; they are complete nonsense. It is nothing other than complete stupidity because it is really comparing apples and pears. We should ask ourselves very seriously: how is it that the human being can be the focus for other human beings? And every human being is a centre for others, making the person at one and the same time centre and periphery. There is only one answer, and the answer is as follows: because the child, after it is born, acquires the skill of walking, speaking and thinking during the first three years of its existence; this is how man becomes a human being among human beings. Just think about it — no animal *learns* to walk, to speak and to think, only the human being. For the human being these three years are set apart, as it were. One does not learn to walk and speak and think merely in order to able to say 'I' to oneself at the end of the third year; rather does one learn to walk, to speak and to think in order to create the psychosomatic conditions for becoming a human being among other human beings.

The human being lifts himself into the vertical position, thereby creating the basis to meet other individuals. Then he learns to speak — only with the help of others — and through speaking he can communicate with other human beings who also walk and stand upright. Then the child learns to think; this enables him not only to communicate but to convey what he is experiencing as an individual. If you picture this vividly in your imagination, dear friends, you will see that the power of uprightness, which enables the child to stand and to walk, makes it possible for us to form a human society of individuals. The fact that we are able to speak makes it possible for these individuals to communicate with each other, and thinking makes it possible for this communication to become an interchange between I and I. These are the prerequisites for the formation of a human society. All this takes place during the first three years of human existence.

The consequence is that the first three years of life are those that prepare the child for becoming a member of humanity. As human beings we are born out of the isolation in which we existed in our mother's womb, where we were nothing but isolated beings in the process of becoming, given over to cosmic powers, wrapped up in our own karma: this is how the human being is born. But this is a germ, and this germ unfolds, leading to the development of walking upright, of speaking and communicating, to thinking and communing. From this arise the preconditions of social life. But we know that something else develops from walking, speaking and thinking. From walking arises the sense of word that enables speech to develop. Speaking leads to the development of thinking, which in turn leads to the development of the sense of thought or concept. Thinking leads to the development of the sense of 'ego,' the perception of the

'I' of the other person, and from this arises the knowledge, the immediate, sensory experience that the other person too is an individual. So walking, speaking and thinking — these are the prerequisites for a social organism. It is the sense of word, the sense of thought and the sense of 'I' that make possible communication within a social organism. The animal cannot walk upright, nor speak, nor think. This is a fact that should be clear to science today.[1] What is not known, however, is that the next step, namely the acquisition of the sense of word, of thought and of I, the three highest human senses, do not exist to enable us to live on earth as individuals, as isolated individuals within the earthly realm, but that by means of the three higher senses we may be able to communicate with our fellow human beings. Out of this arises the social organism. Unless you can come more and more to the clear inner experience of the fact that the three higher senses, the study and knowledge of these three higher senses, is the precondition of all community, of social community, those things I tried to indicate at the beginning will not reveal themselves. Often we use words, and there is nothing behind them; we need to begin to fill these words with real life.

Let us now ask ourselves what it is that is given to us within social life through the sense of word, the sense of thought, the sense of I. What do I experience in the other person through the sense of word? Everybody should ask themselves the question: what do I experience through the sense of word when I am together with the other person? I experience that the other person speaks, be that in words or in gestures. I experience through the sense of word that the other person is speaking. That is, I know immediately, without having to think about it — because it is a sense perception — that the other person too is a speaking being. This signifies something quite extraordinary. It is the power of uprightness which causes a sense to awaken in me which tells me whether the other person is capable of speech or not, whether he is or is not a bearer of speech. This is a vital perception, and it is only through this that we are able to discern the elements of social life. It is through the sense of word that I experience that the other person is speaking.

Through the sense of thought I do not experience *that* the other person is speaking, but through the sense of thought I experience *what* the other person is saying. This means that I understand. The sense of word does not enable me to understand; it only tells me that the other is also a talking, a speaking human being — that he is endowed with the miracle of speech. The sense of thought, however, reveals to me immediately what the other person is saying. The fact that some of you *understand* what I mean is the function of the sense of thought. The fact you know *that* I am speaking is due to the sense of word. For this constitutes the bones, muscles and nerves of social life. I am able to live in the social realm together with other people through the fact that I experience that the other person speaks. However, actually understanding what the other person is saying is sometimes much more difficult.

And what about the sense of I? The sense of I enables me to perceive the I of the other person. This is a sense of its own. The sense of I not only enables me to know that the other is there, to be satisfied that the other is at least as tall or as short as I am. The sense of I does much more than that. If someone were to speak a sentence such as, 'The moon is shining brightly tonight,' and we were to begin by listening with our sense of I (from which nobody can escape), then we would notice how, through diction and tone, through the phraseology, rhythm and melody of speech, the I of the other person reveals itself. This can only be grasped through the sense of I. These infinitely subtle variations, which can only truly be grasped by that great artist, the sense of I, reveal to us the I of the other.

This progression of senses provides the preconditions for the establishment of a social community of whatever kind that is not just a tribal community based on blood ties. It is clear that we establish a society by means of the higher senses on the basis of thinking, speaking and walking.

Now I shall digress a little in order to give you a brief glimpse behind the scenes of creation. What is the source of these three senses? They originate from a single source, which metamorphoses, and this source is the faculty of hearing and the ear. The sense of word, the sense of thought and the sense of I all arise from the sense of hearing through the fact that the power of uprightness begins to work in the ear, that speech makes use of the sense of hearing and that thinking too is connected with hearing. In this way it becomes clear that the ear is the social sense organ *par excellence*. Time and again I have to refer to a statement made by Rudolf Steiner, according to which the ear existed before the human being did. The ear was the first to exist, and the human being arose from the ear.[2] This means that we can say that the true ear, true hearing comprises the totality of all human beings. The same does not apply to the eye, because the moment the human being went through the Fall, his eyes were opened. Just as it is the eye that isolates, it is the ear that communicates. While we cannot withdraw from hearing we can close our eyes. Through our ears we are tied to our surroundings, to our environment and to the whole of humanity. The ear makes accessible to us everything happening around us. The eye does not do that; rather, it obscures the truth. Through the eye we behold — and this should not be overlooked — the wonders of the external world of *maya*. But what is behind it, the being of the other, is revealed to us through the ear. The ear is the archetypal organ of the social human being. It cannot be stated more clearly than that.

Having taken this step, it is possible to go a little further. We can now ask ourselves, where is the sense of word at work, where is the sense of thought at work, where is the sense of I at work? Here we encounter another threefoldness. The sense of word works in the nerve-sense system, and through the fact that it works in the nerve-sense system it gives us the perception that the other person speaks. The sense of thought works in the middle system, and through this middle system we learn to understand, to comprehend, to grasp what the other or the others are saying to us. But the field of activity of the sense of I is the limb-system and to a certain extent also the metabolic system. Thus we have a sense of word, a sense of thought and a sense of I. Let us again pose this question, what do we grasp by means of the sense of word? We perceive language as language. That means: just as I can grasp the human being as a human being, in the same way can I grasp through the sense of word that language is language; this is due to the sense of word. The sense of thought or concept enables me to grasp the message that is being communicated to me within the language. This means, no longer simply the language as language, but language as communication. And the sense of I, as I said, conveys to me the language of the other I. It reveals to me the other I *through* the language. These are the three realms of language. These are the three realms of the sphere of language which builds the bridges, weaves the threads and clears the paths from one human being to another.

It is language — not the activity of speaking — that actually permeates the entire social organism, the human being among other human beings. One could almost say that just as the blood pulsates through the human organism, so language pulsates through the social organism. Just as no human being would be able to live without streaming blood, so no social organism could be without the flow of language. Just as the blood is continually changing, so language too is in a continual process of change. From year to year the language among nations, among peoples, among small groups of people is transforming. If you were to walk through Überlingen today with a discerning ear in order to hear how an Überlinger speaks, and if you were to walk through Überlingen again next year, you would notice that it has changed; it has become different, albeit not very much. Of course today we are so crude, so narrow-minded that we are not aware how language is in a continual process of change. I can remember, for example, how during the war I would occasionally listen to German radio, just out of interest. Then I realized that I no longer understood the German language, that it was something completely different, I could not immediately come to terms with it, I had to get used to it gradually. Because we are always in the middle of this process, we do not notice it. It is really very different hearing the German language in Germany today from what it was ten, let alone thirty years ago. This is not a characteristic of the people speaking but of language itself.

Let us now make these things a living reality so that we become conscious of the fact that we are not isolated human beings, but that we are embedded in the currents of social life as much as we are in the currents of the etheric, astral, cosmic forces. The social realm is not an intellectual edifice constructed by economics professors. The social realm is one of the most real conditions in which people are embedded, and it is maintained and enlivened by the pulse of language. The sense of word reveals to us language as language. It reveals to us that the other is my brother, for he too speaks. This means that we are brothers because the other speaks. Just as we both speak, we also both work, be it with our hands, our brain or through language. The speaking man is also the working man, and as a working man he produces, he promotes, he forms, he acts. This we do as human beings alongside other human beings. Ploughing, cultivating, sowing, spinning, throwing pots, sawing, hammering, pounding. All this is the manifestation of language as language. Now the fact begins to become understandable, that the economic life belongs to the realm of the sense of word or speech. The economic life, in which I do things, in which I speak, is the sphere of production; here we stand next to each other, human being next to human being, brother next to brother, upright, one next to the other, and we grow into it as walking human beings. This is the sphere of the economic life.

Walking — sense of word — economic life — brotherliness

However, where language becomes understanding, where the sphere of the sense of thought begins to work, where I no longer stand with the other, upright next to him, where I speak with the other and he must begin to understand me, that is something completely different, that is something mutual — the fact that I speak and the other understands what has been said. Here we don't stand next to each other, but we stand facing each other; one facing another, one facing many, or many two by two, it doesn't matter. This is the sphere of rights. This is where *verdicts* are pronounced.⋆ This is the sphere of speaking, where human beings communicate with one another and understand what they are saying to one another.

Speaking — sense of thought — rights sphere — equality

And finally, when language becomes the revelation of the other I, when we grasp hold of the sense of I, we establish the sphere of the free spiritual-cultural life.

Thinking — sense of I — spiritual-cultural life — freedom

We have now advanced a good deal further, so that we see, or can at least intuit, that in the sense of word the economic life unfolds. We could also say with full justification that out of the economic life that we share together as human beings, out of the brotherliness of being together, and out of the uprightness of being together, our sense of word is born. We can go further and say: out of that sphere, in which the life of rights has to establish itself wherever human beings are speaking with one another in such a way that an understanding arises between them, in other words, where the sense of thought is present, there we live with others in the sphere of rights.

You see how these things become real, how these things are

⋆ *Verdict* is from Middle English *verdit,* truth spoken.

not artificially thought out. Suddenly out of the mighty ear of the whole of humanity there arises the active human being, the economic life; the human being who understands other human beings, the life of rights; and the human being who reveals himself to others through language, the free spiritual life. The essential point is that we now know that it is these three higher senses that make us into a *zoön politikon*. The human being is not isolated, and the reason he is not isolated is that he is is able to walk, speak and think, because he has the sense of word, of thought and of I. All this now begins to become alive because it is in the context of the human being.

The human brain is constituted in such a way that it carries the sense of speech and of word, the sense of thought and the sense of I. These are imprinted into the brain. The human brain does not grow so much larger because the human being is so much cleverer than the animals. This is complete nonsense; animals are far cleverer than human beings. The knowledge of the human being cannot be compared with the wisdom of animals. Spiders with their webs, wasps with their nests, bees with their hives, beavers with their dams — these represent exceptional wisdom compared to which we are an ignoramus. But the fact that we have such a large brain enables us to become a human being among other human beings.

Rudolf Steiner once told us how these three faculties of the small child — the powers of uprightness, speech and thinking — are only made possible through the power of Christ beginning to work in every single child during the first three years.[3] After that it withdraws again. This means that we receive the foundations of our social existence out of the powers of Christ. These powers create walking, speaking and thinking, faculties which enable us to become social beings. Following on from this, the sense of word, of thought and of I arises as an emanation, as an outpouring of what may be called the Holy Spirit. This streams into the entire social sphere in which our lives are immersed. Once upon a time, thousands and thousands of years ago, the human being was capable of perceiving the spiritual worlds, of supersensible perception, of looking into the depths of the heavens. This faculty was lost in the course of Atlantean times, and in its place human language formed and developed. Speech arose because clairvoyance was lost. For instance, in the chapter 'Our Atlantean Forebears' in *Cosmic Memory,* Rudolf Steiner describes how the awakening of language led to the formation of states in Atlantis. Society arises out of language, but it developed — take this as a picture — because the heavens withdrew their wisdom. What was lost reappears as social life on the basis of language.

The social structure of humanity becomes more and more apparent from century to century, and now the time has come when it needs to divide into what represents sense of word, sense of thought and sense of I, in other words, into economic life, the rights sphere and spiritual life. And each of these three areas has to be filled with this new spirit, with the healing spirit, with the Holy Spirit. The important insight that we should strive to develop is that peace, peace among mankind, can only be attained when an understanding is gained of the new spirituality that fills the society, the community life of human beings. We can consider the ground we have covered to be a suitable preparation for Holy Week. We shall take the next step on Easter Sunday.

VII.

Nun aber erkennen wir:

Die Christus-Kräfte, die im kleinen Kind
das Sehen, Sprechen & Denken ermöglichen,
sie wandeln sich in den drei obersten
Sinnesorganen zu den
Kräften des Heiligen Geistes um.
Dieses aber ist die Sphäre des sozialen Lebens.

Einstmals, da waren die Menschen noch
hellsichtig; die geistige Welt war ihnen eine
Realität. Das verging;
Als Kompensation des Hellsehens
entstand die Sprache

Aus Sprache & Schrift
entwickelte sich die Gemeinschaft
im sozialen Leben.

Nun muss der individuelle Mensch
sie durchgeistigen, damit der
neue Geist,
der heilende Geist
darin erwachen kann.
Einzug in Jerusalem.

*A page of Karl König's preparatory notes for the Palm Sunday lecture.
He would always make detailed notes but then speak freely. For these
first three lectures there were 22 pages of notes.*

Wonder, Compassion and Conscience
The New Garments of Christ

Fourth Lecture
Föhrenbühl, Easter Sunday, March 29, 1964

Dear friends,

Previously we have endeavoured to attain a certain kind of insight into what Rudolf Steiner described and proclaimed as the threefold social organism some decades ago — more than four decades ago, in fact. Initially we approached these ideas from a historical point of view. Then we gained a quite fundamental insight into the connection between the human being and the social organism. In fact we came to recognize how right Aristotle was when he described the human being as the *zoön politikon*. We even had to admit that the human being is only truly human when he lives and works in community with others. That he cannot attain to his humanity on his own; were he to grow up on his own he would not have the possibility to become a speaking being, a being expressing himself through speech, which means that he would not be able to develop thinking, and that probably after a while he might even lose the power of uprightness he had previously attained. In formulating it this way, I am referring to something quite basic, and that it is the fact that it is in the first three years of human life, when the human being learns to stand upright, when he begins to speak and on the basis of his speech unfolds his thinking, that — in contrast to animals — he becomes a human being among other human beings.

This is something so essential that I believe we will have to inscribe it more and more into our hearts: the fact that the human being who walks and stands upright is rooted in the economic life, that the speaking human being exists in the rights life, while thinking man is the being who, in community with others, establishes the free spiritual life. This was the first step we made, and this was followed immediately by a second, namely, that the three spheres of society — the economic life in which things are processed, manufactured, produced; the life of rights, in which human beings meet one another as equals; the spiritual life, in which each one is free to create spiritually while still co-operating with others — that these three spheres do not exist independently of the individual human being, nor do they arise, as it were, through people's mutual co-operation. It is rather that these three spheres arise from qualities of the human being which Rudolf Steiner referred to as the three higher senses.

Perhaps it can be understood when I say, the human being is only complete when he is socially active. The human being is only complete when he begins to realize that his higher senses reach out in a certain way into the social environment. The sense of word or speech creates the economic life, the sense of thought shapes the life of rights, the sense of I permeates the sphere of free spiritual life. I will give one or two examples to illustrate what I mean. Some vertebrates give us a kind of picture — albeit in a materialized, hardened and narrow form — of what I have just tried to hint at with regard to the human being. For example, when fishes build their nests in the water, when birds form their nests, when beavers make their dams, this cannot be seen as something that takes place outside the animal realm. The reality is rather that the formative forces of a bird stream outwards at certain times of the year, creating not only wings and beak, but also fashion a nest according to its particular species, shape and nature. Whether it be a nest made of sand, of mud, of leaves, of soil, a round nest, a rectangular one or an oblong one, it is part of the bird, it is part of the swimming fish, it is part of the ingenuity of the formative forces of the beaver. It is part of the animal rather than part of the social organism; the formative forces, which encompass more than the actual body, are here externalized. Something similar, one might even have to say, the same process but on a higher level and in a different realm, takes place in the social sphere: the sense of word, which grasps language as language, gives shape to the economic life; the sense of thought, which grasps the content of what is being spoken, penetrates the life of rights; the sense of I, which grasps the other human being directly as an individuality, constitutes the spiritual life. This is the picture we managed to build up together last time.

Then we may have started to have a fundamental experience of the fact — without which it is impossible to grasp the nature of the social organism — that a state, a people, a community, a village, a town is not merely the sum-total of all the people living there, hundreds or millions of them, but that it is a higher organism not made of flesh and blood, but is made up of qualities of form, of souls and spiritual faculties. Wherever the same language is spoken, an organism arises, in which the different organs take the form of diverse dialects. Quite distinct form gestures develop in each of these dialects. This is not merely a case of one human being imitating another, but formative forces are at work here, etheric forces which make it possible for language to be recognized not merely as language but as meaning. The more we begin to see this as a soul-spiritual organization, the more will the economic organization, the rights sphere and the spiritual life as described by Rudolf Steiner come alive for us.

But you see, all this did not exist right from the beginning; it has taken thousands upon thousands of years for such soul-spiritual forms of social life to emerge. And it was always,

always, dear friends, language that created the preconditions for such forms. We can look back, for example, to the beginning of Atlantean times, when bodies were constituted very differently from what they are today, where everything was still alive and malleable. Then the human being was barely capable of bringing forth a word. But there were sounds within the evolving souls, into which language was gradually being implanted step by step by the powers holding sway in history. As a result of this the various original Atlantean tribes gradually began to speak. At the same time the first group formations arose. This was not just a parallel development, but a causative process. Not merely within tribes on the basis of blood ties, speaking human beings began to communicate with their brothers who spoke and understood the same language, and together they formed a group. In such a group there was always one who spoke best and who at the same time also had the strongest memory. On the basis of his memory and his ability to speak he would become the leader. Later on, memories and experiences were transmitted to children and grandchildren by means of language, and in this way tribes based on a common language were formed. This represented not only the formation of a community, but it meant that the community was handed down from generation to generation through language. This was the beginning of an emergent rights life and as yet it was nothing more than that. Certain individuals did have something like a spiritual life, but this still took place completely in the lap of the spiritual world. And the earth itself constituted the economic life; it was not the human being but the earth that formed and produced. This is how it was at the beginning of the development of humanity, when people came together in groups more and more.

With the onset of the post-Atlantean age things began to change slowly, but very slowly, as for the majority of human beings social life was not conscious at all. A few individuals were the rulers: the king, the military commander, the priest. And it was the priests who led the economic life, for they indicated when the sowing should be done, when the harvest should be gathered, and they indicated the way this or that musical instrument should be shaped. All this was the activity of the priest. The military leaders dispensed justice, and the kings and bards provided the myths through which people nourished their innermost spiritual needs. At that time differentiated social spheres did not yet exist. There were indeed bearers, seeds of a conscious social life. Of course there were warriors, these were integrated into the rights life; there were arable farmers, cattle breeders, artisans, and they were integrated into the economic life, and there were a few scattered artists and bards, master builders who were integrated into the spiritual life, but this still constituted an entirely natural order of things. The power of uprightness and the sense of word were completely interwoven with them, as was speech and the sense of thought as well as the sense of I that was active within them.

People only really woke up to a conscious social life in the Greco-Roman cultural epoch. It was in the fourth post-Atlantean epoch, which began around 747 BC, that the Greeks and the forerunners of Roman culture awoke to the realization that man was a social being. This was the beginning of an impulse that in our time is attempting to break through in a revolutionary manner in the form of a new social order.

This was the time of attempts at a *res publica,* and experiments with city states such as Athens, Sparta and Thebes, where people felt themselves called upon to participate in their city, in their country, and to take part in military campaigns in support of their country. This is when Cato committed suicide because the political forms which Caesar was creating no longer corresponded to his own. Just imagine this, how vital the feeling for political forms were! This was only possible because just at that time something completely new had taken place within humanity.

In those centuries before the Mystery of Golgotha, around the seventh to fifth centuries BC, something entirely new took place.

Karl Jaspers (1883–1969), a great modern thinker, pointed to this 'nodal point of history,' and wrote a whole book about it. But Rudolf Steiner had already pointed it out previously, describing how suddenly in the Far East and in the Near East completely new religions, mighty heralds of entirely new religions appeared, such as Confucius, Zhuangzi (and Taoism), Buddha, but also Pythagoras, the Greek philosophers and the Greek dramatists.[1] Rudolf Steiner pointed out how new qualities were then arising in the human soul, how Greek philosophy, the early philosophers such as Anaximander, Heraclitus and many others only began to think because something had awoken in them, which had previously been completely alien to the human being: they began to marvel, to experience a sense of wonder. Thales marvelled at the world that was opening up in front of him. Rudolf Steiner describes how this sense of wonder arose from the fact that human beings suddenly realized: here I am encountering something in the forms and phenomena of nature that I know; this is something familiar to me, and yet I am at a complete loss how to place it. Read the dialogues of Plato, and you will notice how time and again the foundation of the discussion is this sense of wonder and amazement. What is man? What is beauty? What is love? What is nature, the sky, the stars, the trees, the world, the soul qualities of the human being, what is all this? The earlier spiritual insights had vanished, giving way to wondering reflection. At the core of all the teachings and views of the religions that arose at that time, of Zhuangzi, Confucius, and particularly the Buddha is the teaching of compassion and love. This, too, had hardly existed before. Now human beings began to suffer with their peers, to know of the other, to care for and to live for the other.

And finally — it is almost possible to pinpoint the year it happened — the voice of human conscience awoke. What the early Greek dramatists still represented as the Erinyes, the Furies, later becomes the conscience within. This means that three qualities awakened in the human being: the sense of wonder, from which developed philosophy; compassion and love, out of which arose the new religion; conscience, through which something arises in the inner being of man which began to tame natural drives and desires. This was an enormous step that took place soon after the beginning of the fourth post-Atlantean epoch, that step which in effect prepared the central event of earth-evolution, the Mystery of Golgotha. However, this preparation took place in the inner human being in such a way that conscience, compassion, love and the sense of wonder began to waken within him.

This is easily said, but the question arises: what is conscience? Why do compassion and love develop at that time? What is the sense of wonder, which in the thinking human being stops thinking in its tracks, reins in thought, makes the human being stop short in the same way as the tomb on Easter morning made the disciples stop short when they arrived there. These are not simple questions or problems. Yet I believe that today it is possible to take another step in our understanding, particularly when one begins to have a sense that thereby the human being takes a further step towards becoming a human being within humanity. Man becomes a social being through the sense of wonder at all that is around him, through love for what is next to him, through conscience for what is in him, overcoming the instinctual nature. Just like everything that takes place in human evolution, this too is a step in the gradual process of internalization. Man does not become human by attaining outer perfection like the animals — by having the best muzzle, the best teeth, the best limbs, the most agile body — but by turning his formative forces inwards, not perfecting his physical organs but raising these forces up and transforming them into something new. Children do just that; they do not complete the development of their bones, muscles, organs or tissues as all the animals do: before perfection is reached, these forces are set free and turn into powers of thinking, of speech, of decisiveness, and so on. This too represents a process of internalization. Yet what is it that becomes internalized when conscience arises, when the sense of wonder develops, when compassion and love awaken in the human being? What is internalized here?

It is those three forces that bring about walking, speaking and thinking in the human being that are transformed, metamorphosed and now appear as soul forces. The power of uprightness, through which children in their first year acquire the ability to walk, is internalized, and out of this power conscience is formed. Now a new, an inner power of uprightness arises, through which drives and passions, desires and emotions will constantly be able to orientate themselves, achieving an inner order. If we were to describe this physiologically, we would have to say that the organ of conscience is the heart insofar as the heart is a spatial structure, balancing the three dimensions, holding the centre. It is the heart as a spatial structure that is the organ of that internalized power of uprightness that began to work in all human beings from about the fifth or fourth century BC.

Something similar applies to compassion and love. Children learn to speak; they learn to speak because they have been endowed with that tremendous capacity which we call imitation; soon after birth the child begins to imitate. Just as the transformed power of uprightness becomes conscience, so the transformed power of imitation becomes the power of compassion and love. We can have a sense that this is somehow connected with language, with that sphere which was bestowed on the human being out of the realm of the Logos, so that now the essential core of the Logos, the capacity to love, begins to awaken. Here again the heart is the organ for this, now not in the sense of it being a *spatial* structure, but as that power of the heart which we may call the power of devotion. For it is in fact not the case that the heart drives the blood; rather; the hearts yields itself up to the streaming blood in order constantly to guide it, in order constantly to harmonize it, in order constantly to sacrifice itself to it.[2] It is this power of devotion of the heart that makes it possible for compassion and love to awaken in the soul of the human being on earth.

And what about the power of wonder? As I have already said, dear friends, the power of wonder arises through the fact that thinking is not constantly given over to perception and observation, that it is not constantly submerged in what is provided through experience, that it pauses, grows quiet, looks around, and then stands in awe before the world, allowing it to reveal itself. Here too the heart serves as the organ. The heart, as Rudolf Steiner has taught us, is an organ of consciousness, an organ of waking consciousness. And the heart as an organ of consciousness is the organ through which we experience a sense of wonder. This means that secreted into this heart is the spatial structure, the power of devotion, the faculty of consciousness, and out of these three and together with these three, conscience, compassion and love and the power of wonder unfolded during these centuries before the Mystery of Golgotha, giving human beings an entirely new standing. Man awoke to the consciousness of being a Roman citizen, of being a Greek member of his *polis*. This was an entirely new experience, and if we now follow this process just one step further we come closer to the Mystery of Golgotha and we may have a sense, perhaps even the certainty that this new awakening in mankind of these three faculties had to take place in preparation. These three new human faculties made him conscious of the fact: I am only human through being amongst other human beings; alone I am nothing; alone I cannot be a human being.

Then the Mystery of Golgotha took place, and it did so in a threefold way: first through the events of Maundy Thursday, then through the events of Good Friday and finally through the events of Easter Saturday that led into the mystery of the Resurrection on Easter Sunday.

On Maundy Thursday, Christ sat at the Last Supper with his disciples, broke bread and shared it with them, and blessed the wine, thereby giving himself to his disciples. And then he girded himself with a towel and knelt in front of each disciple to wash his feet. Through his sacrifice and through his actions, Christ permeated the conscience emerging in the circle of the disciples, and through the circle of his disciples the whole of mankind. On Maundy Thursday conscience is Christianized. And because in Judas the voice of conscience was silent, he was cast out of the community into the dark night of loneliness and solitude. At the same time what gradually appeared later as economic life is permeated by Christ forces in the image of bread and wine. Christ said, 'He who ate my bread has lifted his heel against me' (John 13:18), for he will become the Lord of the earth, on which we all walk and tread. This earth is both the foundation of all the production and generation as well as the body of Christ; it is that bleeding and wounded head that we all tread when we walk, in awareness of the truth of the words: 'He who ate my bread has lifted his heel against me.' But into this event resounded the clatter of the thirty pieces of silver. The same thing is still happening today. Anyone who sells, or is forced to sell, his labour for money in an immediate sense becomes a follower of Judas. Christianized conscience begins in the realm of brotherhood, which is only slowly emerging in economic life.

Then Good Friday followed, where Christ was put on trial and judgment pronounced, he was sentenced to death, and that sentence was carried out. Yet it worked on: this sacrifice permeates the sphere of rights with compassion and love, Christianizing it in the process. Because Annas, Caiaphas and Pilate experienced neither love nor compassion, they were the outcasts. Pilate's question, 'What is truth?' is completely beside the point. What was at stake was not truth, but recognition born of compassion and love, and this was lacking in Pilate, the Roman citizen. It was also lacking in the Pharisees and the Sadducees, and therefore the trial took place that culminated in the image of the cross.

Then on Easter Saturday all outer work ceased. The trial too had ended because the Sabbath had arrived. The image is now the tomb. The dawning light of the Resurrection began to light up the earth and to enter single individuals such as Nicodemus and Joseph of Arimathea.[3] They began to feel deep wonder;

they began to arrest their thinking. Even some of the Jews had a strange feeling because everything was so quiet. The disciples were gathered together in the Upper Room, and they too did not understand what had taken place. They lacked a sense of wonder. However, in such men as Nicodemus, a Pharisee, and Joseph of Arimathea, an Essene, there arose a sense of wonder similar to that of the Greek philosophers, only now it had become Christianized and had as its focal point the tomb, from which no voice, no sound was heard.

Thus economic life, the life of the rights sphere and spiritual life became Christianized by the events of these three days: through the humility of Christ, through the sacrifice of Christ, through the light of the Resurrection which is beginning to shine and is trying to awaken a sense of wonder in human thinking. But what does this mean? In a very special lecture in 1912, Rudolf Steiner revealed something that is of the greatest importance for the future of mankind. He revealed that the astral, the etheric and the physical nature of the Resurrected Christ are woven out of the human soul faculties of wonder, compassion, love and conscience, which have arisen since the Mystery of Golgotha. Rudolf Steiner expressed it in the following words:

> The power of wonder and amazement about things,
> everything that can live in us in the form of amazement
> and a sense of wonder, which has unfolded since
> the fourth post-Atlantean cultural epoch within the
> development of mankind which started with the Mystery
> of Golgotha, all this ... helps to form the astral body of
> the Christ impulse. Everything in the nature of love and
> compassion which comes to life in human souls, forms
> the etheric body of the Christ impulse, and what lives
> in and inspires human souls as conscience, since the
> Mystery of Golgotha until the time when earth evolution
> will have reached its destination, forms the physical body,
> or its equivalent, for the Christ impulse.[4]

The power of uprightness that is internalized to form conscience, is carried through the sphere of production and is Christianized. At the end of earth evolution this will be the physical form, the body for the Christ-Spirit. The transformed faculty of imitation, when filled with the power of the Logos, becomes compassion and love. This weaves and threads through the life of rights, weaving the etheric form for the Christ-Spirit. And the sense of wonder of the thinking human being in the spiritual life, where thought itself is halted, will form the astral body for the Christ-Spirit. So that it is possible to affirm that in the social realms, in which we human beings become truly human when we are able to Christianize them, we will weave the New Earth, the New Jerusalem. Immediately following on from the above passage Rudolf Steiner quotes the Gospel of Matthew (25:40):

> A certain passage from the Gospel only now gets its true meaning: 'As you did it to one of the least of these my brethren, you did it to me.'

In the Gospel of St Matthew (25:35f) Christ stands as the judge of the world at the Last Judgment, separating the sheep from the goats and saying to the sheep: 'I was hungry and you gave me food. I was thirsty and you gave me drink ... I was naked and you clothed me.' This is indeed what we can do as human beings when we marvel, when we allow those faculties to speak in us through which we weave the garments of Christ with and among our fellow human beings. This is the essential point. Today, on Easter Sunday, it is possible to summarize it in this way (it can also be done in other ways). And it is possible to add the following: what Rudolf Steiner gave us as the Foundation Stone Meditation is designed to help us develop brotherliness, equality and freedom, in conscience, in love and in wonder.[5] 'Practise spirit-remembering' represents the conscience of Maundy Thursday. 'Practise spirit-mindfulness,' is the awakening of compassion and love on Good Friday. And 'Practise spirit-beholding,' is that sense of wonder experienced on Easter Sunday. Then the image of the New Earth, of the Risen One, arises, of whom is said:

> O Light Divine,
> O Sun of Christ,
> Warm Thou our hearts,
> Enlighten Thou our heads,
> That good may become
> What from our hearts we would found
> And from our hearts direct
> With conscious will.

This is the human being among human beings. He can only become a human being through being permeated by Christ, through being led by Christ, a human being who allows the voice of conscience, the light of love and the radiance of wonder to grow in him.

Developing Responsibility in the Social Realm

A Lecture on the Anniversary of Rudolf Steiner's Death

Fifth Lecture
Föhrenbühl, Easter Monday, March 30, 1964

Dear friends,

In many places throughout the world, perhaps in hundreds of different places around the world, people will gather throughout the course of this day to commemorate the anniversary of Rudolf Steiner's death on March 30, 1925. We can vividly imagine how probably on all continents, in North and South America, throughout the whole of Europe, in Australia, South Africa, perhaps here and there in Asia, as individuals or in groups, people remember Monday, March 30, 1925. We can form an impression of the increasing extent to which anthroposophy has become implanted in the fabric of human existence. I believe it is important that we try to keep imagining where, how and in what way anthroposophy has become alive and has been taken up. Relative to the present world population, the numbers who have taken up anthroposophy is small, and yet the actual number today is considerable. Here we may think of the spread of Christianity, which grew from a very small number to the point where almost every human being on earth knows or senses what is meant by Christianity.

The same thing applies to anthroposophy because we need to realize that the spreading of that spiritual seed that became active through Rudolf Steiner, is developing further despite all opposing powers, both within and without, despite the enemies of anthroposophy and often even despite its representatives. In expressing something like this, the intention is not to condemn, but to point to the phenomena, so that we can say to ourselves that however inadequate our actions are, whatever our errors of omission, anthroposophy is growing. People come, ask questions, seeds are planted in human hearts, and begin to germinate. Some whither away, some continue to grow, some begin to flower, a few bear fruit, spread new seed, and this way progress is made, and anthroposophy acts as a leaven within humanity today.

We need to inscribe into our hearts the knowledge that despite all failure anthroposophy continues to spread its roots, its branches, its flowers and that it has become effective. There is only one thing we need to pay attention to in this context, in my opinion, and that is, that we should make an effort to recognize those forces in ourselves and around us that again and again set themselves against the spread of anthroposophy. We should not look for these in particular associations of people (although they are particularly active in certain groups), but they are liable to be active in ourselves, in every one of us, unless we focus on them continually and try to recognize these forces of retardation for what they are.

Rudolf Steiner drew attention to them time and again, and yet time and again people have failed to see them and have fallen for the manifold temptations so prevalent in our age.[1] If we try to characterize these counter-forces in some way, we find that they manifest in three different guises. One of these is Jehovism, and by Jehovism I mean that power which, as a unitary godhead, once led the Jewish people and inculcated in this people, with justification at the time, the belief that they were a chosen people. This lives on today. It not only lives on in the Jewish people, it lives in all people. It lives first and foremost in the German people, who are still deeply attached to Jehovism, to the belief in being a chosen people. It is alive in Americanism, it flourished in French nationalism, in Protestantism, it lives in Catholicism. It is alive wherever a people or a world view is so filled with self-belief that it tries to encompass the whole world, that is, wherever we find a sole deity with the character of a Father God who wishes to obscure the being of the Christ, of the Son, and thereby the Holy Spirit as well.

Apart from Jehovism, centralism is one of the greatest enemies of anthroposophy. Wherever centralism tries to spread, where a small group endeavours to achieve control, where individuals are deprived of the opportunity of making their own decisions, wherever all threads are meant or are forced to come together in a centre, be it a state or an industrial enterprise, a religious community or whatever, wherever centralism — and this is the case everywhere nowadays — raises its head in any kind of communal organization, where centralism endeavours to hold sway, the activity of anthroposophy as a seed force is made impossible.

The third guise is nationalism. Wherever nationalism arises — and it is beginning to take hold in ever new human communities, be they peoples or states — wherever nationalism manifests, it is bound to ally itself with centralism and Jehovism; it is these three which are opposed to anthroposophy,

This not only applies to 'them,' this tendency is found in every one of us. The human being naturally has centralist, nationalist, Jehovist tendencies, and every day, time and again, we have to try to counteract these tendencies, to escape centralism, to abjure Jehovism, to condemn nationalism in and

103

around us. The fact that despite anthroposophy hundreds of people can have a nationalist, a centralist, a Jehovist outlook, only goes to show — not that we or anyone of us is better than the others — but what it is that lives in everyone of us as a counterforce to true spiritual cognition. This can also be regarded as the animal in us and in our age; as those beings that are described in the Apocalypse, for example, and in many other places. Wherever anything in us is convinced that it is entitled to wield centralized, national, Jehovist power — and are we not all so convinced in some recess of our existence? — we need to be aware: this is the opponent in us. This is the opponent in us for the reason that it runs counter to the essential mission of anthroposophy, the spiritual science of Rudolf Steiner.

When I say, the essential mission of anthroposophy what do I mean? There is really only one word to express this. Because the essential mission of anthroposophy is the permeation of all existence with the new Christ impulse. Whoever tries to push this aside, to deny it, has already fallen victim of centralism and Jehovism, for Rudolf Steiner has pointed out, not once, but time and again, that spiritual science wishes to be, tries to be, one with the mission of Christianity itself. This must not remain mere lip service, this must not remain empty words, it must be put into practise. It only becomes real, it only develops further — and thank God it is developing further — where we allow the Christ impulse to come to expression within our initiatives.

It is easy to speak of anthroposophical medicine; this is beginning to develop here and there. But an anthroposophical doctor is not someone who knows how to apply the seven metals, when to prescribe Infludo and Cardiodoron and when not, anyone can do that, so to speak. However, one only becomes an anthroposophical doctor when one endeavours — and many do that — to transform one's medical thinking through the Christ impulse to such an extent that silver and gold, incense and myrrh begin to come to life in one's soul, and then become effective in conversation with the patient and the therapeutic intervention. Eurythmy is not only a new art but it will really only become an art when the eurythmist develops the capacity to know that it is the Christ impulse which is beginning to be active in it. Even the religions, be they Christian or otherwise, are bound to perish, despite conclaves and huge missionary gatherings of hundreds of thousands. Such initiatives are wonderful, and they are justified — and yet unless this new element of the Christ impulse begins to awaken, and unless in the realm of scientific experiment the laboratory table becomes an altar, unless in the realm of philosophy the sort of Pauline thinking awakens which is beginning to unfold for example in Rudolf Steiner's *Philosophy of Freedom;* when in the realm of agriculture Christian prayer is not offered to the ground of the earth, then anthroposophy will remain sterile. When I suggested that we remind ourselves how this day is commemorated in so many places across the whole earth I was trying to indicate that anthroposophy has not remained sterile in many hundreds of places.

With regard to Rudolf Steiner, whether it be his life, his death or his work, we have to recognize that what was working through him was the Christ impulse which he wanted to implant right down into human social life. This may come to expression sometimes within the family, in human communities, or it may come to expression in the individual human being, but wherever it may be, it is important that we recognize it for what it is. Rudolf Steiner said in a lecture:

> [Christ] himself said — I have often quoted it: 'I am with you always, even unto the end of the world.' This means: Christ did not speak only during his time on earth; his utterance continues, and we must continue to listen for it. We should not wish merely to read the

gospels (though they ought to be read over and over again); we should listen to the living revelation that springs from his continued presence among us. In this epoch he declares to us: 'Make new your ways of thinking' (as his forerunner John the Baptist said: 'Change your thinking'), so that they may reveal to you man's threefold nature which demands also that your social environment on earth shall have a threefold membering.[2]

The Christ impulse longs to take shape and to be fulfilled right down into the historical-social realm. And in this lecture Rudolf Steiner points to two ways in which the human being today can serve the Christ impulse. He spoke here about a path of thinking and a path of will. It is one of those lectures he held in 1919 before an audiences of many hundreds, proclaiming the new order of social life and describing the phenomenon of mankind's approaching the threshold of the spiritual world in this century. Today it is possible to say that humanity has indeed reached that threshold and is performing this dreadful dance at the edge of the abyss. He describes how the human being can become a servant of the Christ both in the realm of thinking and of will, and appeals to them to do so:

> This is possible only if we know that the human being living since the Mystery of Golgotha has a certain defect, for which he must compensate through his own activity during his life here on earth.[3]

Rudolf Steiner points out that belief in God is a natural thing for every healthy human being, and that only a person who is sick, truly sick, can deny the words, *ex deo nascimur* (we are born out of God), but that this no longer suffices today and that something else needs to arise in us, and that is the knowledge that we are born with a predisposition to being ruled by prejudice. He expresses it in the following way:

> I am born a prejudiced person, and freedom from prejudice in my thinking is something I have to achieve during life.
>
> And how can I achieve it? The one and only way is this: instead of taking an interest merely in my own way of thinking, and in what *I* consider right, I must develop a selfless interest in every opinion I encounter, however strongly I hold it to be mistaken. The more a man prides himself on his own dogmatic opinions, and is interested only in them, the further he removes himself, at this moment in world-evolution, from the Christ. The more he develops a social interest in the opinions of other people, even though he considers them erroneous — the more light he receives into his own thinking from the opinions of others — the more he does to fulfil in his inmost soul a saying of Christ, which today must be interpreted in the sense of the new Christ-language.
>
> Christ said: 'Inasmuch as ye have done it to one of the least of these my brethren, ye have done it unto me.' The Christ never ceases to reveal himself anew to human beings, even unto the end of earthly time. And thus he speaks today to those willing to listen: 'In whatever the least of your brethren thinks, you must recognize that I am thinking in him; and that I enter into your feeling, whenever you bring another's thought into relation with your own, and whenever you feel a fraternal interested for what is passing in another's soul. Whatever opinion, whatever outlook on life, you discover in the least of your brethren, therein you are seeking myself.'

This is an extraordinary statement. When Rudolf Steiner says something like this, we can be sure that he himself is listening at the heart of the Christ, hearing Christ speak as he calls out to human beings: 'Through the least of the thoughts of your fellow man that you accept, through the interest you develop for the least thought of your fellow man, you accept me together with him.' Dear friends, if only we could be ever mindful of this when we notice that yet again we have been too ready to judge instead of listening to what the other has to say, even if he appears ever so stupid. It is not necessary to agree with the other, one can have one's own opinion, but one should not represent it in a centralist, nationalist, Jehovist way. One can listen, hear, express appreciation in the knowledge that the Christ thinks in the other at least as strongly as he thinks in me. Rudolf Steiner continues:

> If I do not look on myself alone as the source of
> everything I think, but recognize myself, right down
> into the depths of my soul, as a member of the human
> community — then ... one way to the Christ lies open.
> This is the way which must today be characterized as
> the *way to the Christ through thinking*.

This is one thing. Rudolf Steiner speaks about the path of will in the following way: what takes place nowadays in the education system seems all too often designed to destroy the motivation and enthusiasm of young people or — as some of us or most of us have experienced — to whip it up in a particular direction. However, this enthusiasm alone is no longer the most important thing. Rudolf Steiner calls it youthful enthusiasm, youthful idealism, which needs to be replaced by something new.

> Something further is required — idealism must spring
> from inner development, from *self-education*. Besides the
> innate idealism of youth, we must see to it that in human

society something else is achieved — precisely an *achieved enthusiasm:* not merely the idealism that springs from the instincts and enthusiasm of youth, but one that is nurtured, gained by one's own initiative, and will not fade away with the passing of youth. This is something that opens the way to the Christ, because — once more — it is something acquired during the life between birth and death.

Feel the great difference between instinctive idealism and achieved idealism! Feel the great difference between youthful enthusiasm and the enthusiasm which springs from taking hold of the life of the spirit and can be ever and again kindled anew, because we have made it part of our soul, independently of our bodily existence — then you will grasp this second idealism, which is not merely the idealism implanted in us by nature. This is the way to the Christ through *willing,* as distinct from the way through thinking.

This is in fact one of the many aspects which Rudolf Steiner has made available to us for the attainment of the true mission of spiritual science. And this true mission of anthroposophy is identical with a renewed Christianity. This is a fact that cannot be denied, which cannot be shaken, as it would mean denying or shaking the truth of anthroposophy. It may enable us to feel that we live here on earth not merely boxed in between birth and death, because the pre-birth existence radiates into the life of every human being; the sun-radiance of after-death existence reaches into every human being. This is to enable us to experience that we do not reach perfection between birth and death, but that we are spiritual beings surrounded by hundreds and thousands of other spiritual beings on this as well as on the other side. The consciousness or at least the assurance or at least even just the intimation of an awakening to the experience of a spiritual world can only be the result of this renewed Christ impulse. At the end of the 1890s Rudolf Steiner had the profound experience of 'standing in the most solemn celebration of cognition,' through which the Christ impulse was revealed to him.[4] What arose for him from this experience was — whether we like it or not — the sole source of anthroposophy. And anthroposophy is alive, alive in the light-wings of the Risen One.

Rudolf Steiner concludes the exposition cited above by addressing the sense of responsibility for everything we think and do which must arise from this:

> [We must ask ourselves] can I justify ... [what] I am doing or thinking ... in the light of my responsibility towards the supersensible spiritual world? Can I justify it in the light of my knowledge that everything I do here on earth will be inscribed in an akashic record of everlasting significance, wherein its influence will work on and on? Oh, it comes powerfully home to one, this supersensible responsibility towards all things! It strikes one like a solemn warning, when one seeks the twofold way to the Christ — as though a being stood behind one, looking over one's shoulder and saying repeatedly: 'You are not responsible only to the world around you but also to the divine-spiritual, for all your thoughts and all your actions.'

This is the essence of anthroposophy.

> But this being who looks over our shoulder, who heightens and refines our sense of responsibility and sets us on a new path — he is the one who first directs us truly to the Christ, who went through the Mystery of Golgotha. It is of this Christ-way, how it may be found and how it reveals itself through the being I have just described, that I wanted to speak to you today. For this

Christ-way is most intimately connected with the deepest social impulses and tasks of our time.[5]

This should be our commitment: to call to mind ever anew, dear friends, that when anthroposophy is true to its own nature it is identical with the new Christ impulse.

Michaelmas and the Threefold Social Order

Three Lectures

Föhrenbühl, Germany, Michaelmas 1964

The Spiritual History
of Central Europe
and the Threefold Structure
of Karlstejn Castle

First Lecture
Föhrenbühl, Sunday, September 20, 1964

Dear friends,

On our recent trip to Bohemia it was really the visit to Karlstejn Castle that made the deepest impression on us.[1] As I have been studying both the building itself and the history of this castle for a long time — in fact over thirty years — I thought that I might say something about its history as well as its significance and position within the spiritual life of Europe. Rudolf Steiner also referred to it now and then in private conversation. He said, for instance, that Charles IV, the builder of Karlstejn Castle, had been 'the last initiate on the imperial throne.'[2] During a visit to the Karlstejn — as far as I can remember it was in 1920 in the company of Count and Countess Poltzer-Hoditz — ascending the staircase to the chapel of the Holy Cross with them, he pointed out that the wall paintings along the staircase, ostensibly depicting scenes from the life of St Wenceslas and his

Karlstejn Castle.

grandmother St Ludmilla, were actually scenes illustrating the Chymical Wedding — evidence of the fact that this 'last initiate on the imperial throne' had still been able to give shape and form to this castle on the basis of spiritual insight.[3]

Now, many people who visit this castle, upon entering one chapel or another, one room or another, or passing through this or that particular door, may find themselves inspired by a sudden spiritual insight, while others, perhaps hundreds of thousands, walk through and it means nothing to them. And so this building has stood for 700 years, one might say, at the very heart of Europe, and yet it still appears as chaste and untouched as ever. It is almost impossible to grasp that the stern clarity of its structure, the austere beauty of its form has been preserved in its original state. This was also the impression we received this time, despite the terrific crowds. The guide told us that every year now hordes of people — some quarter million in fact — are herded through, and yet none of the spiritual magic of this castle has been lost.

From whichever side one approaches the castle, which is situated to the west of Prague, one initially follows the Beroun valley and then ascends, finally reaching a landscape of hills and woods, and suddenly the castle appears, the central tower and the other surrounding buildings, high up on a limestone outcrop, inaccessible from north, west and east: a magical structure. One asks oneself what makes it so magical. It is bare, square and nevertheless quite extraordinary.

It is important to look at the historical background of the creation of this architectural structure. The Karlstejn was built in 1348, more or less exactly in the middle of the fourteenth century. And what does this fourteenth century represent? The Karlstejn forms part of a tremendous building drive, which emanated essentially from the personality of Charles IV. At the same time as the castle, a particular part of Prague, the so-called Lesser Town (Malá Strana) was built. Charles IV saw to it that the powerful artistic personality of Peter Parler* was given the opportunity of building St Vitus' Cathedral, Prague Castle was enormously extended, the Charles Bridge across the Moldau (Vltava) was built in the heart of Prague. All these buildings still exist today. If you walk cross the Charles Bridge, so massive, wide and powerful, you find it hard to imagine how such a structure, so full of formative strength, could have been built seven hundred years ago. And as you walk across the bridge, the Castle and St Vitus' Cathedral gradually come into view in front of you. However, this development was not confined to Prague. St Stephen's Cathedral in Vienna, for example, was built at the same time, as was Freiburg Minster and Cologne Cathedral. All these buildings arose from the Gothic style and yet they were no longer typically Gothic, leading already beyond the peak of this style, from its flowering in the Middle Ages, into that curious,

---

* Peter Parler (1333–99), was apprenticed with his father in the craft of cathedral building at Cologne. He completed Karlstejn Castle, which had been started in 1334, after his predecessor, Matthias of Arras, had died without leaving any building plans.

extraordinary fourteenth century, when old forms were disintegrating while new ones were being prepared but could not yet reach perfection.

It was also at this time, in 1348, that the first German university was founded by the same Charles IV in Prague. Soon after, in 1365, the university of Vienna was founded and very quickly, only a few years later, the university of Krakow. You can see that in the fourteenth century the centre of gravity of the sciences, of theology, of medicine was shifting from the west and the south of Europe to the east. In the thirteenth century the university of Paris had still been the centre of all knowledge and scholarship, the place where Thomas Aquinas, Albertus Magnus and all other eminent scholars taught. A short time before that, Chartres, to the south of Paris, had been a centre of medieval spiritual life. Italy too already had universities. But now suddenly the east was beginning to wake up. At the same time the Order of Teutonic Knights was spreading eastwards, towards the Baltic regions, towards Poland, towards East Prussia. Here you see as one of the characteristics of the fourteenth century the fact that Central Europe was no longer confined to the Rhine, which until then had been the scene of all important developments; now Bohemia, Hungary, Poland and the Baltic regions began to wake up. After he had become Holy Roman Emperor in 1346, Charles IV had been the first to move the centre of the Reich to the east of Europe. Prague became the capital of Europe for the first time, and around this centre things began to unfold.

At the same time the first precursors of what would later become known as humanism and the Reformation developed in several places. The period between the end of the thirteenth and the beginning of the fourteenth centuries saw a towering figure such as Dante; and we can hardly mention Dante without remembering his contemporary, Giotto. What emerged here simultaneously represented the conclusion of the Middle Ages and the emergence of the modern age of that epoch. For immediately following Dante came Petrarch and Boccaccio, those two great Italian poets, writers, who were in fact already beginning to develop and express their thoughts and feelings in a kind of modern spirit. Reading the *Decameron* or some of Petrarch' writings where for the first time an attempt is made to transform Greco-Roman cultural elements into European-Italian ones, it is noticeable that the all-encompassing thought cosmos of someone like Dante, which still had the quality of a macrocosm, had come to an end. Mankind was beginning to acquire new faculties.

Now we know from Rudolf Steiner that around the middle of the thirteenth century, in approximately 1250, a mighty incision took place in the spiritual life of mankind.[4] This incision marked the end of the possibility of immediate and direct spiritual knowledge. In the middle of the twelfth century the walls between the physical and the spiritual world became impermeable, as it were, and personalities such as Thomas Aquinas or Albertus Magnus were no longer able to gain even the slightest insight into the spiritual world. What they did was to create a world view by their own efforts of thinking. But imagination or even inspiration was no longer accessible. The sunset of a final direct perception of the spiritual world is represented by Dante in magnificent beauty. The last remnants of direct, immediate medieval spirituality now came to an end. Human beings woke up into a kind of self-knowledge and lost the last vestiges of spiritual perception, which had previously lived in them as an intimation of spirit vision.

When a process such as this takes place, we usually find that a certain seal is impressed upon it. In the middle of the fourteenth century a terrible seal of this end of the Middle Ages was impressed upon European humanity. That seal was the plague, which at that time was called the Black Death. I believe that today we cannot even begin to imagine to what extent this plague ravaged the population. Starting in Constantinople in 1347, it spread via Messina and Venice through the whole of Italy, swept through Switzerland and Southern Germany into

France, Northern Germany, Bohemia and up to the Baltic countries, to Britain and Ireland, right up to Iceland, to Greenland. In Central Europe itself many millions of people perished in just a few years. It is estimated that around a quarter of all Europeans — whole generations, fathers, children, mothers — particularly in the towns but also in the villages were exterminated by this plague. Outbreaks recurred in the fifteenth, sixteenth and seventeenth centuries, but did not take hold of the population to anything like the extent it had done in the fourteenth century.

It is interesting to characterize this disease, at least tentatively. It is an epidemic transmitted by rats and fleas. We should contemplate this fact a little. The fleas get the plague bacillus from the rats and transmit it to humans. This means that the lowest form of animal existence, the most devilish form of animal existence becomes the carrier of this epidemic. The fleas transmit it to humans. Wherever the fleas bite, boils develop, which ulcerate. However, the centre of the plague attack is the lung, the organ that, according to Rudolf Steiner, represents the earthly, solid element in us, and it is precisely this organ that is destroyed.[5] So, during the very time when people became bearers of sense-based earthly thoughts, millions were exterminated by this merciless disease, which had its origins in Tibet. We should really explore this in detail some day.

At the very time when the emergent humanism of the fifteenth and sixteenth centuries was foreshadowed in the work of Petrarch and Boccaccio, there were also precursors of the Reformation. From a historical point of view something very interesting now emerged: the close relationship between England and Bohemia; the spiritual relationship between England and Bohemia became visible. The Reformation really began with John Wycliffe. Wycliffe was born in Yorkshire in the 1320s and some time later he became Professor of Divinity at Oxford University. Oxford was already a famous university at a time when in Prague the university was just beginning. And Wycliffe was one of the first to harbour doubts about Church

Christianity, which had become pompous and rigid, as well as about the priesthood and the supremacy of the Pope. He turned against celibacy and expressed doubts about the transubstantiation in the sacrament of communion. He said — and this was one of his main teachings — that the Church should not really be a visible institution at all, but that the Church was for him nothing but 'the invisible community of those who are predestined for beatitude or the blessed life.' It is so important to see how a new living spirit, a new way of thinking in the direction of community emerges in that century. The existing institutions are typical for the end of the Middle Ages, being outwardly fixed by rules, vestments and statutes. Now a man appears — and it is significant that he should be an Englishman — who asserts that the true Church is not the visible one but the invisible community of those predestined for beatitude, for the blessed life. At the same time his awakening thought life makes him doubt transubstantiation. What possible basis could he have had for comprehending and affirming it?

Now John Wycliffe had a follower called Jerome who was born around 1365 or 1379 and later, having become a teacher of divinity, became known as Jerome of Prague. He studied Wycliffe's ideas at Oxford and took his teachings over to Bohemia. There is a connection here. He was a friend of the great reformer Jan Hus. Together these three, Wycliffe, Jerome of Prague and Jan Hus, constitute the actual protagonists of the fourteenth century pre-Reformation. We should not forget that both Hus and Jerome were burnt at the stake just across from us in Constance: Hus in 1415 and Jerome in 1416.* This was at the time of the Council of Constance, which took place between 1414 and 1417. The fact that these two men, who aside from Charles IV can be regarded as the leaders of the Czech-Bohemian awakening, were

---

* Constance is visible from Föhrenbühl across the Lake Constance on clear days. Thirty years after his death Wycliffe too was declared a heretic by the Council of Constance in 1415. His works were condemned and his bones burnt.

burnt in this area by the Catholic Church, is a significant part of the fourteenth century.

This was not the only significant development. Apart from what we can see as an influence on building, on religious life, on literary and artistic life, below the surface of outer spiritual life, a new stream emerges. This new stream emanates exclusively from the Dominican Order. This stream first arose in the thirteenth century, coming to a flowering in the fourteenth century, and that represents the flowering of German mysticism. It began with Meister Eckhart, who sat at the feet of Thomas Aquinas and Albertus Magnus. He had absorbed a new kind of Platonism, and with direct spiritual perception being no longer possible, he had been able to kindle within himself the spark of divine light through inner schooling, through spiritual schooling. He calls this light his 'tiny spark,' the eternal light that every human soul can kindle within. He had pupils, who were also Dominicans. One of them was Heinrich Seuse (or Suso), who lived between 1295 and 1366 either here in Überlingen or in Constance, it is not known exactly which; he was an extraordinarily lovable personality, unbelievable in the degree of his spiritual cognition, but at the same time extremely clear and incisive, who wrote the first German autobiography. If you would like to get a feeling for the spirit of this region, I would recommend you read this autobiography or even the autobiography of Charles IV. Then there was the greatest of the three, Johannes Tauler, 1300–1361, whose formidable activity was based in Alsace and in Strasbourg and in Basle. These three Dominicans, who worked through sermons streaming from their innermost soul, represented a further source of the developments that took place in the fourteenth century.

It is known that, particularly through Tauler, mysticism was linked to that subterranean stream in history connected with the activity of the Friend of God, that exalted personality who was none other than the great Zarathustra.[6] He would appear again and again throughout history as a leader of humanity. Through the cooperation between the 'Friend of God' and Tauler, the mighty preacher, something of what was working secretly in the background at the heart of history during that time became visible to those who had eyes to see.

Up to the twelfth and thirteenth centuries — perhaps until 1220 or 1230 — it was still possible for earnestly seeking pupils to find their spiritual teacher. Rudolf Steiner once described in a heart-moving way how such meetings would take place, how the eye of the teacher could perceive the pupil, leading to immediate spiritual cognition.[7] We learn further how the pupil was then led to an experience of the spirit of his youth, the spirit of his old age, and how he thereby discovered, through direct experience, that the other world is real while this world is unreal. This possibility came to an end around the turn of the twelfth to the thirteenth centuries, ceasing completely. The time in which people were still able to have direct spiritual meetings had passed. From then on individual spiritually striving personalities would gather together, praying, meditating, seeking one another in community, resulting in an extraordinarily intimate mood taking hold of such small circles of people, in which supersensible beings could appear to them, not physically, who would say to them, 'Through your humility, through your prayer, through your devotion you have called me.' Dear friends, this is how from the end of the thirteenth century right through the fourteenth century, those beginnings were made which were the seeds of what later became Rosicrucianism.

Here I would like to quote a passage from a lecture by Rudolf Steiner:

> Now something else developed within this endeavour of spiritual research, of spiritual cognition. It is something extremely beautiful to behold when one sees: Here are three brothers and four others, three brothers who are only able to succeed in making a meaningful contribution to the world if the other four work together with them.

They are completely dependent on one another. The three are able to receive revelations from the spiritual world while the other four are able to translate them into ordinary human language. What the three are able to give would remain completely unintelligible pictures if the other four were not able to translate them. And on the other hand, the four would have nothing to translate if the three did not receive their revelations from the spiritual world in the form of pictures. As a result of this something developed within such communities, which particularly in those centuries was regarded by certain circles to be among the very highest human achievements: an inner brotherhood of soul, a brotherhood of cognition, a brotherhood of spiritual life. Through their striving in this regard, such small circles came to experience the real value of brotherhood. Gradually they began to feel more and more strongly that in the course of humanity's development towards freedom the bond between human beings and the Gods would be completely severed unless it were maintained through this kind of brotherhood, where one person is truly dependent on the other.[8]

Now in these small brotherhoods three would sometimes go out, as it were, and in so doing would receive spiritual revelations in the form of images, bringing these inner pictures back with them. The other four would translate these pictures into signs, into the language of the time and were thus able to communicate and utilize them. And we must imagine one group and another and a third and fourth and fifth group — often knowing nothing of one another — some perhaps living in a town, others moving from village to village, healing the sick and preparing for what would later, in the fifteenth and sixteenth centuries, come together in the secret order of the Rosicrucians. These were the three and the four.

All these phenomena, dear friends, form part of an under-standing of the inner nature of the fourteenth century. But what was happening outwardly? I shall just highlight a few develop-ments. Switzerland became a confederation in 1381. The State of the Teutonic Order developed in the East, as I mentioned earlier. At the close of the Middle Ages the important ruling dynas-ties and their outer influence also came to an end. Henceforth there would be no more Ottonian (Saxon), Salian (Frankish) or Hohenstaufen emperors; all this had come to an end; only one or the other of the diverse lineages would ascend the throne. Charles IV was from Luxemburg; his predecessors had been a Bavarian, an Austrian, a member of the Habsburg family. The succession was no longer predetermined.

Charles IV was a great organizer and builder; he now instituted something that, in my opinion, has been completely misunder-stood: he created a completely pragmatic law that has entered the annals of history as the Golden Bull. This is a law regulating the election of the Holy Roman Emperor. The remarkable thing about it was that it stipulated that the seven so-called Electors have the right to appoint the emperor. This means that there was no longer a hereditary succession based on the bloodline, but the seven have the task, as it were, to choose the most suitable per-son. In reality they did not do this in most cases, but at least that was the intention. And who were these seven? These seven were three spiritual leaders and four secular rulers. In this, Charles IV acted out of an awareness of the small inspired circles active in the background of historical developments, and this is what he wanted to bring to the fore here. The three spiritual leaders were to receive the inspirations while the four secular ones were to translate them and turn them into practical action.

The three were the Archbishops of Mainz, Trier and Cologne. The four were the rulers of Saxony, Brandenburg, the Palatinate and Bohemia. Now it may seem strange, but it was one of the remarkable insights of Charles IV that there were three arch-bishops to represent the world — of the three diocese, Cologne stood for Italy, Mainz for Germany and Trier for Burgundy — and four secular lords. They were the Lord Cup-Bearer, the Lord High Steward, the Lord Marshall and the Lord Chamberlain. Now of course this did not mean that they served wine and food to the emperor and kept his rooms tidy, but it meant that they represented the power of the wine and the power of the bread, the altar and the vestment. This means that the spiritual realm and the earthly realm are intertwined in this Golden Bull. At the core of all this is the wellspring of the Rosicrucian impulse which I have already mentioned.

All this underlies the building of Karlstejn Castle. That is the actual spiritual foundation of this building. Historians and anybody else who tries to explain the Karlstejn, or who writes about it, would say that the reason it was built so solidly was to safeguard the crown insignia and important state documents behind strong walls. Of course, outwardly this is quite right and yet at the same time it is wrong. Charles IV was in fact an initiate on the imperial throne, and while his endeavours were premature, he saw the role of the emperor as the representative of the spirit on earth. His insignia were kept in this sacred Christian space; state documents were drawn up and signed in this same sacred space. This was the intention and purpose for which the Karlstejn was built.

Perhaps I can now give you a brief description by way of an overview of the castle itself. Approaching the Karlstejn, one sees various structures. The very highest structure is a square tower (C in the diagram). This tower is connected only through a small wooden bridge with another building (B), somewhat larger, situated a bit lower down and also isolated. This building in turn is connected through a corridor and gallery to a much larger building (A). These are the three main buildings.

The entrance is through the first gate (D), and there is a second gate (E) before one comes to a large courtyard. The whole thing has a strange layout, resembling a kind of snail-shell, which has as its midpoint the tallest, central structure. The building

Plan of Karlstejn Castle

A Imperial Palace
B Lady Chapel
C Holy Cross Chapel
D First Gate
E Second Gate
F Well House
G Burgrave's Palace

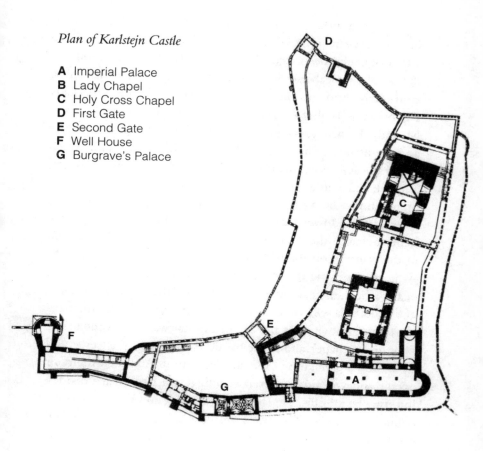

adjoining the courtyard (G) was the apartments or palace of the burgrave of the castle. It has nothing to do with the castle itself. In front of the Imperial Palace (A) there is another courtyard with a spring that still runs today, enclosed in a brick channel deep underground. The whole structure is built on rock. Everywhere you can see rocks showing through.

The large building (A) is the Imperial Palace, containing both the private apartments, and the small St Nicholas Chapel (at the lower right of A) for the use of the imperial family and its entourage.

Walking a little further, you come to that part which consists of two sections. One of these is the Lady Chapel (B), which was originally decorated with wonderful representations of the whole Apocalypse. Unfortunately only traces of it can be seen today. And this little side chapel here, adjoining the Lady Chapel, was built for Charles IV. He would go there every Maundy Thursday, staying there until Easter Sunday, in prayer and meditation. There was only a small hatch, through which important state documents would be passed for signature, as well as drink and a little food. During this time he would not see any other human being face to face. From there you go up to the tower. In this tower there is a long flight of steps leading to the highest chapel, the Chapel of the Holy Cross (C). The left side of the stairway on the way up shows scenes from the life of St Wenceslas: sowing the corn, harvesting the wheat, the threshing of the wheat, the baking of bread. And on the other side the life of St Ludmilla, where she is picking grapes, pressing them, making them into wine. At the top of the stairway you come to the door of the chapel, and above the door you see St Wenceslas and St Ludmilla partaking of the chymical meal. And then the door opens, and you find yourself standing in a large space divided into two by a trellis, the larger one in front and the smaller one behind the trellis. The walls are clad in malachite and inlaid everywhere with magnificent precious stones: carnelian, topaz, beryl, etc. Above, the walls are covered with portraits of saints painted by the great painter of the time, Theodoric of Prague.* There are about ninety saints altogether. The fact that behind each of the saints a relic connected with that saint was let into the wall has largely been forgotten today.

In the smaller space there is an altar. And above the altar — this is the chapel of the Holy Cross — relics from Golgotha were set into the wall. So you can actually feel yourself surrounded —

---

* Theodoric was court painter to Charles IV, working 1359–68; he was the master of the Prague Guild of Painters. The paintings in the chapel of the Holy Cross are the only surviving traces of his work.

and if you want to, you can still experience this today — by the sacrifices and sufferings of so many important saints. Something quite extraordinary seems to be living and weaving in this space. Along the wall there were chests in which the documents relating to the Golden Bull were kept, while behind the altar the imperial insignia were kept locked away.

So the Imperial Palace (A) is the building pertaining to the life of the body; then on entering the Lady Chapel (B), people could more and more experience the life of the soul. Ascending to the highest, to the Holy Cross (C), to the Holy Spirit, something was enkindled which was the fire of the Holy Spirit. This is one aspect of the Karlstejn. Next time we shall look at the castle in connection with the threefold social order.

In conclusion, I would like to point out something particular. This fourteenth century, which we have endeavoured to understand is actually framed by two events of great importance for mankind: one of them occurs in 1314 and the other one in 1413. In 1314 the last Knights Templar were burnt at the stake together with their last Grand Master, Jacques de Molay at the instigation of one of the most evil spirits in history, Philip the Fair of France.* Through this event the Middle Ages were extinguished by means of fire and the sword. Then something new began to stir: the early precursors of the Reformation, of humanism, the early beginnings of Rosicrucianism and of mysticism, leading to the year 1413, when when a new age dawns, when the age of the consciousness soul begins, in which we are still living today. The fourteenth century, framed by these two events, is the age of Charles IV who was born in 1316 and died in 1378.

In the same year, in 1378, Christian Rosenkreutz was born again, began his journeys to Holland, where he became a monk, travelled from there to Damascus, Arabia, Egypt, absorbing the last remnants of eastern spirituality, and returning in 1459 he founded the Rosicrucian Order. In this order are gathered

---

* In fact the ones who had gone to Scotland and lived around Camphill were never burnt. This was not known to König.

together the many small springs of the brotherhoods of seven that I described earlier. At that time the Reformation as well as humanism were unleashed. It was also the time when the printing press was invented: a completely new epoch began to gain momentum. Something momentous was happening here. Yet the inner spirit of continuity was preserved. Whether this would be sustainable in the long run nobody could say at the time. The matter was settled in the fourteenth century. The person who helped on the one hand to externalize it, yet preserving its inner essence, was Charles IV, and Karlstejn Castle bears witness to this. It is still possible to experience this today if we approach the building with an open heart. One can still sense the spirit of Rosicrucianism hovering over it. Walking through those gates one can sometimes have the feeling: Christian Rosenkreutz himself passed through here.

The Michael Festival as a New Festival of Community

In Memory of
Rudolf Steiner's Last Address

Second Lecture
Föhrenbühl, Monday, September 28, 1964

Dear friends,

It is forty years ago today that Rudolf Steiner spoke to a larger circle of people for the last time. This was on September 28, 1924. Already in great pain and seriously ill — after an immeasurable amount of work and countless lectures in the preceding weeks — he once more gathered his forces to give an address. He told his audience that the approaching Michael mood, 'which shall radiate from this day into tomorrow and the days following' — gave him the strength to speak once more. Many of us here have made it a custom to read this address at Michaelmas and perhaps on other occasions throughout the year. Whenever one reaches out inwardly to what is here being said, tries to approach it, something quite particular arises in the soul. For these words engender a particular mood. Everything Rudolf Steiner said here was permeated by a mood that we can only describe as one of sorrow, as a mood of farewell. Those who were present at that time confirm this, independently of one another. It is in fact the same mood of farewell which one can experience outside in nature at this time of year; that farewell which allows a gentle feeling of sadness to arise in the soul; a sadness which is deeply connected with the experience of the approaching autumn season.

However, within the sorrow that resounds through Rudolf Steiner's words there arises an impression of understanding filled with hope. And within the mood of farewell that comes towards us, something comes to birth that one can only describe as the germ of resurrection. In what is coming to an end there lives the germ of resurrection. And what is the essential message of this last address? Rudolf Steiner looked back once more to the beginning of his activity in the cause of anthroposophy, to the year 1902, in which he gave the lectures later published as *Christianity as Mystical Fact.* The significant thing about this book is that at its centre the personality who was the author of the Gospel of St John, Lazarus-John, is mentioned by name more or less for the first time. This is expressed in this book, which was Rudolf Steiner's first book about anthroposophy in simple but unambiguous words

At the end of the wealth of lectures bestowed on us through him in the year 1924 — there were nearly eighty karma lectures — at the end of all these lectures Rudolf Steiner once again refers to the being who represented the beginning of all his karma research: the being of Elijah-John. In these karma lectures Rudolf Steiner had traced the destinies of leading personalities of the past, particularly of the nineteenth century, back to their previous incarnations. In this way another arch is stretched, reaching across to Lazarus-John, because in his last address Rudolf Steiner revealed for the first time that the individuality of the Baptist and the Apostle are intimately connected to the extent that after his death the Baptist's individuality works through the Evangelist. In this address Rudolf Steiner then traces the path of this being through the Christian era, where he becomes the painter Raphael and who then, not so long ago, was the poet Novalis.

The extraordinary thing about this address is that the period from 1520 to 1772 — from the death of Raphael to the birth of Novalis, about 250 years — is allowed to pass before our gaze. Rudolf Steiner opens the gates for us, as it were, and allows us to follow the path of this soul through the heavenly planetary spheres. At the end of this lecture Rudolf Steiner issues an appeal: now he suddenly tells us how necessary it is that human beings should come forward, that human beings who would be leaders of true Michaelmas festivals should join together. Let me read you the relevant passage:

> If in the near future, in four times twelve human beings,
> the Michael thought becomes fully alive — four times
> twelve human beings, that is, who are recognized not by
> themselves but by the leadership of the Goetheanum in
> Dornach — if in four times twelve such human beings,
> leaders arise having the mood of soul that belongs to the
> Michael fesival, then we can look up to the light that
> through the Michael stream and the Michael activity will
> be shed abroad in the future among mankind.[1]

The fact that these were among the last words spoken by Rudolf Steiner to the community of members of the Anthroposophical Society: a call to community building around four times twelve people — a community building impulse under the sign of a Michaelmas festival renewed out of the Spirit — this fact we should really inscribe into our hearts. Rudolf Steiner impresses the closing words of this address like a seal upon what is to come, as it were, the words of that great Michael meditation which begins:

Springing from Powers of the Sun ...

This is what can be described as the essential message of the Last Address. If, looking back on the preceding months, we see this address as a kind of crown, we become aware of how, from about April or May of the previous year 1923, with ever increasing intensity, Rudolf Steiner directs our attention towards Michael, towards the significance of Michael for our time, which is to awaken in us the endeavour to become pupils of Michael.

On May 23, 1923 in Berlin Rudolf Steiner gave a special lecture where for the first time — as far as I can see — he pointed with this sense of urgency to the need for the institution of a renewed Michael festival. If we look at this lecture — it was the last one Rudolf Steiner held in Berlin, and so it was also a farewell, and once again sorrow sounded through this lecture — we can become conscious of the following. Rudolf Steiner began the lecture by referring to the destroyed Goetheanum. He spoke in deeply moving words about the fire. He said very significant things about it, and I would like to quote one sentence:

> Even if some kind of building for our purposes should arise on the same site — which should definitely come about — it cannot become a full replacement of the old Goetheanum because of the difficult circumstances of our time.[2]

And then he broke off and went on to speak at length about the development of walking, speaking and thinking in the first three years of the child. The incarnating soul is endowed with the faculty of walking, the faculty of speaking and the faculty of thinking through spiritual meetings and spiritual experiences before birth. On coming to earth from the spiritual word, these faculties then awaken in the small child as true humanity. He spoke at length about sleeping and waking, about death and rebirth, and then — at the end of an extraordinarily long lecture filled with all the recent discoveries of anthropsophy — he suddenly refers to Michael and to the Michael festival, which at that time did not yet exist.

There were of course traditional Michael festivals. Religious calendars carry the word 'Michael' against September 29; these were really peasant festivals, but the fact that a Michael festival once stood behind the harvest festival had been completely forgotten by most people.

We would have to go far back into pre-Christian times to find that resurrection festivals were celebrated in the mysteries during the autumn time of the year. But now something new was to be started, and I need to read you some passages from this lecture, because they are the original words that were to lead to the renewal of the Michael festival:

> If we are conscious of the secrets of the earth's circuit during the course of the year we know that the Michael power is now descending again through the nature forces, which was not the case in previous centuries. This means that we can now meet the autumn, when leaves are falling, in anticipation of the descent of the Michael power from the realm of the clouds to the earth. Michael now begins to shine through the soul of the earth as it is withdrawing into the body of the earth ...
>
> When, however, the festivals, which today are celebrated without understanding, will again be understood, we will also have the strength, out of a spiritual understanding of the course of the year, to establish a festival which will only begin to have true significance for present-day humanity. This will be the Michael festival in the last days of September, when autumn approaches, the leaves wither, the trees grow bare and nature approaches death — just as it approaches the budding of new life at Easter — when just in the dying down of nature we experience how the soul of the earth is uniting with the earth, bringing with it Michael out of the clouds.[3]

The soul of the earth breathes in, and in our time increasingly since 1879 the Michael power has united itself with this breathing-in — this streaming into the body of the earth, into man's environment and thus into human souls during this autumn season. And this process, which takes place every year but which is mostly overlooked by people because they sleep through it, should bring about something which is described by Rudolf Steiner in the following way:

> For the moment it would be far more important than all
> other social reflections which will only be fruitful in the
> present confused conditions if imbued with spirit, if a
> number of people with spiritual understanding were to
> come together for the purpose of instituting on the earth
> out of cosmic forces something like a Michael festival,
> an autumn festival that would be a worthy counterpart to
> the Easter festival. If something could be resolved upon
> for which the motifs could only be found in the spiritual
> world, and which would create a feeling of fellowship
> among human beings at such a festival, created in the
> immediate present out of the fullness and freshness of
> the human heart, then this would be something which
> could create a social bond among people.

These are weighty words that should be not only intellectually affirmed but taken up into the heart. Only then can they be transformed into action and strength of will.

> In the past, festivals created a close bond between people.
> Just think how much was done, spoken and thought in
> preparation of these festivals and at these festivals for the
> benefit of the whole culture. Because these festivals were
> established out of the direct inspiration of the spiritual
> world, their qualities were imprinted right into the
> physical.

At the end of these deliberations Rudolf Steiner said:

> People would need to find the courage in their hearts not
> only to discuss outer social organizational arrangements

and so on, but to do something which will bind the earth to the heavens, which will again bind the physical conditions to spiritual conditions. Thereby the spirit will once again be introduced into earthly circumstances, and something would really happen among human beings that would constitute a powerful impulse for the further evolution of our civilization and the whole of human life.

Such words make clear the extent to which the proposed Michael festival, which is to be instituted, is to be a festival of community building. Not a festival for the individual who withdraws into himself, but a festival for the individual who wants to be a part of all the others. This is what it is about. If we now look at this lecture as a whole, this last lecture held in Berlin and from which I have quoted, one thing becomes clear: the Goetheanum ceased to exist, and the moment it disappeared, there arose the impulse to establish and institute Michael festivals which were to have a community-building effect. You see, this is the Michaelic insight we should take away from this lecture: the fact that temples, buildings, architectural works of art, if they are authentic, are always connected with occult or public social endeavours. Hence the name Mason, Freemason. The craftsmen, builders, who built the cathedrals, the churches, were only able to accomplish this because they themselves formed part of a guild, for cathedrals and churches are only erected in order to facilitate community. Any group of people who want to become a social community, a church congregation or whatever, will experience the need for a building, or will first erect a building in order to be able to work together in it.

This is one of the secrets of architecture that it immediately brings about social architecture, social structure. And just as the Goetheanum arose and vanished, forms of community should and would arise again out of Goetheanistic impulses. The church as a building unites the community of the faithful. Those who build the church constitute the circle of the initiated. That this is so becomes clear from another aspect of Rudolf Steiner's life work, namely from two lectures held in Stuttgart ten years earlier, in 1913, also in the month of May, where Rudolf Steiner first points to the Michael impulse of our time.[4] He does this at the very moment when the decision had been taken to erect the Goetheanum on the Dornach hill. Thus we can say that the Goetheanum in its inception and its passing is framed by the Michael impulse. The Goetheanum is to be reborn in the Michael festival, creating and forming communities. If this is done in the right way, it cannot be destroyed by fire. This is one thing to which I wanted to draw your attention.

The other thing I wanted to point to is a strange fact which probably belongs to 'reading the signs of the times' which Rudolf Steiner refers to in the opening of the Last Address: on September 28, sixty years before his Last Address, and a hundred years ago today, on September 28, 1864 the first Socialist International was founded by Karl Marx in St Martin's Hall in London. Earlier on, many worker's unions had been established: from the middle of the nineteenth century the awakening proletariat had tried to establish itself as a force capable of shaping history. But today it is one hundred years since an international labour movement was established. This is also an important sign of the times. This event took place fifteen years before the dawning of the Michael age. Workers from all over the world came together, realizing for the first time across the whole world that they constituted a united power. This initiative can be considered a Michaelic one because it transcended nations, and was taken hold of by the will forces of human beings who, with justification, were striving for leadership roles. The fact that things turned out differently is not the fault of the workers; it is the fault of the intellectuals who lead them in an anti-Michaelic manner. It is important to ponder this.

Let us now look back to what I hinted at about Karlstejn Castle. We are dealing here particularly — and in the same way as with the Goetheanum — with a building that was intended to have a socially formative role. It was shaped out of Rosicrucian motivation, it arose out of this Rosicrucian motivation, and the intention was that it should point towards social-political ideals that might have become realized — for example an ideal such as that of the Golden Bull, which I described to you at length last time. It was premature; nobody could grasp it and therefore, as an ideal it had to withdraw again. But this building can be experienced as a threefold structure to this day. There is the Imperial Palace, which saw Charles IV's social activity; there are official reception rooms, private apartments and dining halls, in short, everything that a ruler requires to exercise their worldly power; that was the one building. If we walk through these rooms — even today — we have the feeling: once it must have been filled with everything that the economy, the cultural power and craftsmanship of people could produce in stone, precious stones, clay and other materials. This is the first part.

From this building a little bridge leads to the second, the middle building, which mainly comprised a Lady Chapel, on the walls of which were depicted scenes from the Apocalypse.

From this second building, which stands all by itself, separate from the first and rising above it, another bridge leads to the third building which resembles a square tower, somewhat taller than the second and considerably taller than the first building. On entering, we have to climb a large number of steps with a series of pictures on either side describing the production of bread and the production of wine from the forces of nature through human work. Having reached the uppermost step, we see depicted above the door the chymical meal of St Wenceslas and St Ludmilla. On opening the door we find ourselves in the chapel of the Holy Cross. I have described how the walls are covered in semi-precious stones. On the upper part of the walls there are pictures upon pictures of saints and martyrs. This chapel used to house the documents of the Holy Roman Empire. At the same time it was a chapel for meditation and a chapel dedicated to the Christian ritual.

The configuration of these three buildings points to the three spheres of the social organism. First we have the Imperial Palace, filled with all the goods of the earth, relating to economic life. Separated from, and independent of it, is the second, the Lady Chapel, the sphere of the rights life and again, independent from this, the tower with the Holy Cross Chapel: the sphere of spiritual life. In this structure, which was built in such a mysterious way in Central Europe on the basis of Rosicrucian impulses, the future form of the social order of mankind stands in front of us, prefigured in architectural form.

How can we understand this a little more clearly? We may ask ourselves: when we speak in this way about economic life, when we speak in this way about the rights sphere, when we speak about spiritual life — what is all this in reality? Where are these spheres actually to be found? They do not arise because people work together, or because one group of people pronounces judgment on another, drafts legislation, or because people are artists and poets, scientists. When we ask the real question of where these three spheres are to be found, then here is one possible answer.

The sphere of economics, the sphere of economic life, that is our Mother Earth, for out of the earth, through human labour, everything grows that we need for life. The earth also gives us the water, the stones, the minerals, everything we need by way of clay or fibre; up till now she has bestowed all this on us in never-ending abundance. The fact that a different world has arisen in the last hundred years is no contradiction to this archetypal image that presented itself initially to our perception. Mother Earth is the home of everything that can be described as economic life.

And what about the rights sphere? Dear friends, why is the Lady Chapel decorated with scenes from the Book of Revelation? Because the Book of Revelation depicts the entry of the Logos into the world of the earth and of mankind. The rights sphere is the sphere surrounding the earth, the sphere of language. Here a verdict must be spoken. Hence also the expression 'Judgment is pronounced.' Law and order express themselves in words alone. The human word filled with the word of God that is the law according to which we live and work here on earth.

And what is it that comes to meet us up there in the Chapel of the Holy Cross? There the saints and martyrs look upon us, there those who have died look upon us. For spiritual life, if we understand it rightly, is the sphere in which the dead, in which all the unborn, have their homeland. Spiritual life becomes active where the living communicate with those who have already crossed the threshold or those who are beyond the threshold: the ancient teachers of wisdom who no longer come down to the earth, the angelic beings, the unborn, all this forms the background of spiritual life. And into this sphere Michael radiates and shines, calling to us, gazing at us, waiting for us to recognize him. This is the call that goes out to us today. This is the call that sounds forth from Michael's messengers, who have been sent out to call men to come to the wedding meal (Matt.22:1–14). Then the one goes to work his fields, the other has to give his daughter in marriage, the third needs to fill his purse, and thus for many the call fades away, the call which Rudolf Steiner spoke again in a new form in these verses:

> Springing from Powers of the Sun,
> Radiant Spirit-Powers, blessing all Worlds!
> For Michael's garment of rays
> Ye are predestined by Thought Divine.

Then there appears the countenance that shines through the sphere of the unborn and the dead, saying:

> He, the Christ Messenger, revealeth in you —
> Bearing mankind aloft — the Sacred Will of Worlds;

This is radiant power that appears, and out of the radiance the Logos now streams forth:

> Ye, the radiant Being of Ether-Worlds,
> Bear the Christ-Word to Man.

The Word, the Logos, streams down to men:

> Thus shall the Herald of Christ appear
> To thirstily waiting souls,
> To whom your Word of Light shines forth
> In cosmic age of Spirit-Man.

This is the second sphere; this is describing the second sphere. It calls men to the royal wedding, and turning to men it says:

> Ye disciples of Spirit-Knowledge,
> Take Michael's Wisdom-beckoning,
> Take the Word of Love of the Will of Worlds
> Into your soul's aspiring, actively.[5]

Listen to the call, it says, and come to the table of the royal wedding!

With these words Rudolf Steiner placed into our hands the tools for creating Michaelic communities; to celebrate Michael festivals, not to miss the call because we are asleep, but to meet it with an alert will. This is what matters in our time, which is a Michael age, a time when human beings should never again loose sight of the fact that the newly evolving Michael festival is to become the seed and core of social communities.

Temple Building and Community Building
Goetheanism and the Goetheanum

Third Lecture
Föhrenbühl, Tuesday, September 29, 1964

Dear friends,

Yesterday evening, on the occasion of the fortieth anniversary of the Last Address, which Rudolf Steiner gave on September 28, 1924, we came to the insight that architecture — the style, form and metamorphosis of buildings — is closely and intimately connected with what is built up in the social realm, in short, with what can be described as community building.

This is something extremely important, and it is highlighted for us by the loss of the First Goetheanum. We were able to call to mind how the moment the outer building went up in flames, when the beauty and grandeur of this mighty work of architecture had perished, Rudolf Steiner issued a call for a new direction. That was to rebuild what had perished outwardly as wood, concrete and glass, in a new way so that a new Society, an Anthroposophical Society with new aims could come about. There is an intimate connection between these two events — the burning of the Goetheanum and the formation of the

General Anthroposophical Society through the Christmas Foundation Meeting in 1923. They are as intimately connected as building in stone and building in the social realm has ever been in history. I referred earlier to the existence of masons' guilds; here the initiated carried out the building works so that the uninitiated were able to gather together in common work, in common activity, in building a community, whether through building a temple, an arena, a church or a mosque. This is something we must never lose sight of, particularly during the course of our work together this winter, where we have planned to study the various forms in which communities come about, the formation of social groups who want to work and be active together.[1]

Now another aspect needs to be added which is peculiar to our time. I referred to it yesterday and would like to do so again today in such a way as to allow Rudolf Steiner's words to resound. We described yesterday how after the burning of the Goetheanum Rudolf Steiner wove the light-filled Michael-activity into the building of social communities. The Goetheanum was destroyed. He made clear to us that a new consciousness had to arise for the celebration of Michael festivals, because it is only through the celebration of such Michael festivals that true community building can arise. I will now quote Rudolf Steiner:

> When, however, the festivals, which today are
> celebrated without understanding, will again be
> understood, we will also have the strength, out of a
> spiritual understanding of the course of the year, to
> establish a festival which will only begin to have true
> significance for present-day humanity. This will be
> the Michael festival in the last days of September,
> when autumn approaches, the leaves wither, the trees
> grow bare and nature approaches death — just as it
> approaches the budding of new life at Easter — when

just in the dying down of nature we experience how
the soul of the earth is uniting with the earth, bringing
with it Michael out of the clouds. When we acquire
the strength to establish such a festival out of the
spirit — a festival that brings a feeling of fellowship
into our social life once more — then we shall have
founded something in our midst which has its source
in the spirit. For the moment it would be far more
important than all other social reflections, which will
only be fruitful in the present confused conditions
if imbued with spirit, if a number of people with
spiritual understanding were to come together for the
purpose of instituting on the earth out of cosmic forces
something like a Michael festival, an autumn festival
which would be a worthy counterpart to the Easter
festival. If something could be resolved upon, for
which the motifs could be found in the spiritual world,
and which would create a feeling of fellowship among
human beings out of the fullness and freshness of the
human heart, then this would be something which
could create a social bond among people.[2]

This is the important thing, dear friends, for this is what
was engendered through the architecture, the form of the
Goetheanum. It can only be reborn in the social realm if right
and true Michael festivals are celebrated more and more by
human communities. These considerations, however, have
further implications: That it is not only the building activity as
such which is connected with the social realm, but that with and
within these buildings festivals are celebrated, festive moments
in the course of the year are held in such a way that they can be
inscribed in human souls so that those celebrating together may
form a union, an order, a community.

One of the many reasons why contemporary social life is in
a state of such decline is that we have lost the commitment to

the celebration of festivals in our time; people nowadays actually feel embarrassed at the prospect of celebrating festivals together. With these words of introduction I wanted to round off what I said yesterday.

If we want to take things further, we would now need to look at something else. Let us ask how this Goetheanum was built. In the background we have our awareness of the connection between building and social structures, the connection between social structures and the celebration of festivals within and around the architectural work, so that a social form may arise from it. If we now look back — and in these weeks and months it is just fifty years since the First World War cast its dreadful shadow across mankind — we are bound to see clearly how the Goetheanum arose on an outwardly peaceful island amid the storms of this First World War. This too is an important image for the history of our century, the fact that on an enclave on the Dornach hill near Basle a group of people comprising representatives of all those nations at war with each other were erecting a building together. They were erecting a building from which, after it was finished, a very specific spiritual task was to emanate.

At that time, between 1914 and 1919 something very special was coming into being. Looked at superficially, one might say that it developed in parallel with the coming about of the Goetheanum. If one were to look a little deeper, one would have to say that it arose in the most intimate interrelationship with the development of this building. I shall try to describe it briefly.

In 1916 and 1917 two basic works by Rudolf Steiner were published, which are still very little known, which have not yet even been translated into English, because they have not been taken as seriously as they should have been. *The Riddle of Man* was published in 1916 and *Riddles of the Soul* in 1917.[3] The titles indicate that their author wanted these books to be seen as connected. In *The Riddle of Man* Rudolf Steiner looks back to the nineteenth century, trying to discern threads of true spirituality within the cultural life of that time. He wrote about the three great philosophers, Fichte, Hegel and Schelling, describing them as representing a kind of twilight of the entire spiritual life of Europe, yet already containing the seeds of a new light of the spirit. He went on to describe the extremely significant starting points to be found in the work of a philosopher such as Immanuel Hermann Fichte, son of Johann Gottlieb who, within the framework of his intellectual, yet all-encompassing, consciousness described, almost as a premonition, the entire content of anthroposophy, which was to come in the future. He even used the word 'anthroposophy,' referring to that new spiritualized understanding of man, of which he has a premonition without as yet being able to describe it clearly. Rudolf Steiner then turns his attention to people like Karl Christian Planck and Wilhelm Heinrich Preuss as personalities who have a first dim and semi-conscious perception of reincarnation and karma. He also mentions that within Austrian cultural life there were poets representing spirituality. This is the content of the book, *The Riddle of Man*, and reading it again and again one becomes aware how threads are picked up here which should have formed a bridge to what was to be revealed at the beginning of the age of light as spiritual science.

The other book, published a year later, is called *Riddles of the Soul*. Here a different note is sounded. This is no longer looking to the past but to the future. The book starts on a dissonant note, with a hard and sharp analysis of the work of one of the contemporary psychologists and philosophers, Max Dessoir, which Rudolf Steiner dismisses. Then follows an appreciation of the recently deceased psychologist and philosopher Franz Brentano, about whom indeed an enormous amount could be said as one of the precursors of anthroposophical psychology. Following on this, Rudolf Steiner sketches a new science of man — he himself calls it an 'outline presentation.' Here the twelve senses are described, and the threefold nature of the soul, the threefold structure of the human physical organization are referred to for the first time. The unitary structure of the nervous system not as a motor-sensory but solely as a sensory apparatus is referred to. The nature of the human being is studied here from many other points of view.

What does all this signify? In *Riddles of the Soul* the foundation is laid for a Michaelic spiritual science. And the foundations of this Michaelic spiritual science, this Michaelic science of man, are the essential prerequisites for the idea — that also develops during this time — of the threefold structure of the social organism. All this needs to be seen in its context. It needs to be seen in the context of the Goetheanum, which was in the process of being built and shaped: the Goetheanum, which was intended to be the home of a new Michaelic science of man, a Michaelic natural science. Around this Goetheanum, once completed, something else could have developed, namely the seed of a social organism that would have radiated into the surrounding peoples of Europe.

If we are aware of this, then we can glimpse the divine thoughts connected with the building of the Goetheanum. Here a building was to be constructed: within this building natural science and the entire materialistic knowledge of the time was to be permeated with spiritual knowledge in a Michaelic way. From there messengers were to carry order, social order into the decaying social organism of the time. This decaying social organism had been shaken by the killing of millions in the First World War, had been shaken by the collapse of the moral qualities of the past, had been shaken by the collapse of knowledge of the spirit. These had been the intentions behind the building of the Goetheanum.

This should have been a new start and that would have been possible to some extent, as no clairvoyance is needed for a renewal of a Michaelic natural science. What is required is purely and simply spirit-cognition. Soon after the Christmas Foundation Meeting, on January 13, 1924, Rudolf Steiner tried to describe in a lecture how spirit-cognition became possible in the course of time.[4] At the beginning of this lecture he points out that the time in which we live is a very special one with regard to cognitive possibilities. In earlier times the initiates were able to look at the created world, at creation. In doing so they encountered the active spirit of the creative, formative powers. He described how for example the initiates of the Old Persian epoch were able to look at the forms of the earth and how in these forms — be they animal or plant forms, stones or minerals — how, in these surface phenomena of the earth, they met spirit activity in the form of spiritual images. Later, in the Egyptian period, the initiated looked upon everything constituting the watery element; how in the Greek epoch spirit vision manifested itself through the element of air, like a *fata Morgana;* how eventually, at the inception of the European age, the beginning of the Middle Ages, the last of the initiated — for instance individual Rosicrucians — endeavoured to experience this mirroring of the spirit within the element of warmth. However, as the warmth element no longer permitted this experience, the Rosicrucians had to employ auxiliary means by studying the earthly world, by taking the knowledge into themselves (individuals such as Faust, Paracelsus and others come to mind), and then taking it into sleep, carrying it upwards as knowledge and waiting for the answer from the spiritual world. What they were permitted to know and what was necessary for them to know would then be revealed to them in the form of pictorial symbols.

Rudolf Steiner continues by pointing out that in our time it is no longer necessary to carry this knowledge into sleep, but that by means of particular effort, effort of thinking, it is possible to gain answers in waking consciousness. What one needs to do — and this he calls true spiritual science — is to study modern natural science, taking it into oneself and offering it up to Michael, who will then give back to us this earthly knowledge transformed into spiritual knowledge.

> This possibility still exists today. If you have been touched by this Rosicrucian principle of initiation, you may today study Haeckel's theories with all its materialism, having first permeated yourselves with the cognitive methods outlined in *Knowledge of Higher Worlds*; study everything you can learn about the human ancestors from Haeckel's *The Evolution of Man*, even if it seems repugnant to you, study it in this repugnant form, learn everything you can learn about it from external natural science and then offer it up to the gods, and you will gain everything that is written about evolution in my book *Occult Science*. You see, this is the connection between the feeble, weak knowledge the human being can acquire through his physical body here on earth and the knowledge the gods can give him on the basis of such study, given the appropriate outlook and preparation. Man has to offer up to the gods what he can learn here on the earth, because times have actually changed.[5]

This is what should have taken place within the Goetheanum and wherever the ideals of the Goetheanum were active. Then a comprehensive Michaelic science of man would have been developed. Then the Michaelic messengers would have gone out from the Goetheanum in order to make the threefold social order a reality. The destruction of the Goetheanum by fire was the most terrible historical disaster, as it wiped out the centre of this activity. What was then meant to take its place as a social organism has only been partially effective.

Yesterday I read the passage in which Rudolf Steiner said that no other building would really be able to replace the First Goetheanum. We have experienced the reality of this. But now we have to take the next step: we are still developing our understanding of the connection between architectural building and social building. Let us look back for a moment to that castle, the Karlstejn, in which we could experience an intimation of the image of the threefold social organism. Let us now look from Karlstejn Castle, built in the fourteenth century, to the Goetheanum, which arose in the twentieth century. What does it wish to express? Is it, too, an image of the whole social organism? What is it? We are allowed to ask this; it is not unjustified to ask such questions. What was it intended to represent?

This Goetheanum was intended to be a building of the spiritual life, of that free spiritual life which is a part of the threefold social organism. This spiritual life was to have found its realization in the Goetheanum building. In a lecture Rudolf Steiner called 'Esoteric Prelude to an Exoteric Treatise on the Social Question' he spoke about the background, the esoteric background of the three spheres of social life. He describes the spiritual life as follows. He says:

> Everything ... that gives the human head its configura-
> tion, its form, points to life before birth, points to what
> the human being brings with him through birth into
> this physical life from the spiritual world, either from
> the spiritual world itself or from a previous incarnation
> on earth. Being aware of the connection between all
> individual capacities of the human being, be they manual
> or mental, with the formation of the human head, our
> perception is carried further, so that we are able to
> recognize that everything based on human capacities can
> be traced back to life before birth.
>
> You see what it is that leads the spiritual scientist to
> such a significant illumination of the nature of spiritual
> life in the physical world. Physical spiritual life, my
> dear friends, exists here in the physical world because as
> human beings we bring something with us through

birth. All spiritual life in the physical world, in the sense that I have spoken about today, does not simply arise out of this physical world, it arises from those impulses that we carry from the spiritual world into physical existence through birth. We shape this physical spiritual life in human society here on earth because we are human beings who bring into physical existence resonances of a supersensible existence. There would be no art, there would be no science, there would be no educational impulses, we would not be able to educate the children, we would not be able to give schooling if we did not bring impulses from life before birth into physical life. That is one aspect.[6]

This has to do with the human head, and the fact that we carry a head on our shoulders guarantees the knowledge that we emanate from prenatal existence, that we originate from a pre-birth existence which is much more real than the sense world in which we now find ourselves. It is the guarantee of our spiritual life.

Yesterday I was able to describe to you what is today underpinned by these words of Rudolf Steiner. The actual realm of the spiritual life is that in which the dead and the as yet unborn weave and work. This is the origin of the intentions, and the shape of the Goetheanum is an image, an artistic metamorphosis of this human head. Picture to yourselves once more the ground plan with the large and the small hall each covered by a cupola: the windows, the Christ statue, the pulpit, the pillars — twelve in the small cupola and seven on each side of the large one. This in fact represents none other than the shape of our head.

The small cupola is the forehead, and the large one is the back of the head, the occiput. The windows are like the senses. All this is the architecture, the cosmic architecture that we all carry as effigy of the spiritual activity that took place before birth. And

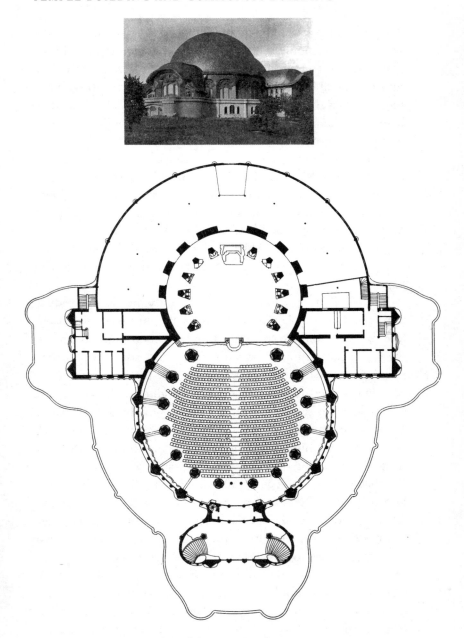

A plan of the First Goetheanum

that the statue of Christ should have stood at the back of the small cupula can only be understood if we remember that in the past centuries an entirely new organ has been formed within the human frontal bone (the part of the skull from the forehead to the roots of the nasal cavity) through the activity of high spiritual beings. In that organ, spiritual cognition, the beholding of Christ in our time, can be born.

This is the ground plan of the building of which mankind has been deprived. Mankind has been deprived of a centre of active spiritual life. This means that the new morality for the sphere of law could not come about as intended and thus could not influence the economic life accordingly. This has resulted in the ongoing catastrophe in which we are forced to live today, and from which there is almost no way out. But what has actually happened?

The economy has gone crazy. Constantly increasing production across the whole world, without true purpose or direction, has led to an explosive rise in the number of consumers, that is in the world population. Production is not increasing because the population is rising, but it is rather the case that more and more consumers need to be born because production has increased so much. What is resulting from this can only be described as a severe asthmatic condition in economic life. Excessive production is like breathing in and breathing in and more breathing in while the breathing out process is missing.

What is it that is being prevented? It is the possibility for human beings to die. Old people are prevented from returning to the spiritual world. They are artificially maintained here on earth as living corpses. This is the result of all the things I have tried to describe to you. Now it is not necessary to say more about it today.[7] But following on from what I have tried to show you, another question can be posed, and that is the following: have you ever really asked yourselves in which style the First Goetheanum was built? Does it stand completely alone within our time, in a vacuum, as it were? Or, if it is a phenomenon of the times — which appears to be the case after everything I have tried to say — where does it belong? You will agree that it is incredibly fascinating to contemplate the various changing architectural styles against the background of the connection between architecture and social form.

Looking back we realize that in the nineteenth century there was no distinctive architectural style. There was a kind of eclecticism. If you walk along the Ringstrasse in Vienna you can experience this very clearly: here Greek, neo-Gothic and Gothic styles have been copied more or less successfully. If it were not permeated with childhood memories, I would have to call it a kind of confectionary style. You will find the same thing in Berlin, Paris, Munich, in all these cities that have been built during the nineteenth century. Going further back, we come to the Rococo, the Baroque; before the Baroque was the Classic style, and the High Gothic; before the High Gothic the Gothic style proper, and earlier the Romanesque or Norman, the Basilicas, and before the Basilicas everything comprising the primitive Christian art of the catacombs, roofed over by the architecture of the Romans with its baths and theatres, circuses and palaces, and finally the Greek temple. We could go back even further, but that is not necessary at the moment.

We should not only look at this but should try to experience it inwardly. How different is a Greek temple from a Roman bath or a Roman palace, from the very early Christian buildings, the Basilicas, the Romanesque style, forever developing further, metamorphosing, forming. All this is accompanied by a transformation in facial expression, gestures, clothing, shoes, thinking, speech, actions, activities — everything is in a permanent process of transformation. It is a continuous process of culture in constant metamorphosis, bringing forth corresponding social forms: from the Greek city states to the Roman Caesars, to the disintegration of all social forms and their reconstitution in monarchy, empire and papacy. If we really picture this vividly, we will realize that at the end of the nineteenth and the beginning of the twentieth centuries a new architectural as well as social style tried to emerge, a style which we can survey in its entirety only now that we have gained some distance from it. It is a style that expresses itself in a similar manner in music, art, drama, poetry and painting — a style which, with a slight note of disdain, we now call Jugendstil or Art Nouveau.

If we now try to identify the people through whom this style came to expression, we notice that all of them were contemporaries of Rudolf Steiner. They were all born at the beginning or in the middle of the 1860s. Be it Gustav Mahler or Henry van der Velde, Gerhart Hauptmann, Eugenie delle Grazie, Emil Nolde or Edvard Munch or Aristide Maillol, in all of them we find this quality of an emergent Art Nouveau which then was not really developed further. Everybody took a bit of it and it became splintered, sexualized, intellectualized, and eventually artists such as Gustav Klimt and Egon Schiele came, who turned what was really trying to emerge into a kind of mannerism. It is interesting to ask oneself where the origins of this Art Nouveau actually lie.

When we ask this question, we are led back to a particular phase that arose around the 1860s and 1850s in England among the Pre-Raphaelites. A certain impetus arose there which lived, for example, in a man like William Morris who had a quite specific intention. He did not merely want to paint a picture or build a house, but his aim was to elevate the entire human life style right down to clothing, interior design and furniture; all these items were meant to embody something new and creative, through which man would become truly human.

But this too was extinguished. It was swept aside through the emergence of the various 'isms': Expressionism, Cubism, and whatever else. However wonderful the individual ideals such as the Blue Rider or the Bauhaus were in themselves — the essence of that Art Nouveau was lost, with one exception, and that was the Goetheanum and everything that began to develop around it as the new Goetheanistic style. Here we have the elevation, the first true spiritualization of Art Nouveau. After the horrors of modern art and the disintegration of all form, this will have to be the starting point for future developments in art. However, this will only be possible after the inevitable ultimate disintegration. Rudolf Steiner indicated precisely the time in which new Goetheanums would arise again all over Europe: in the seventies of the coming century.[8]

If we now look back once again to all those changes in style and ask ourselves, from the point of view of spiritual science, who is behind these changes, we can come to the realization that they are brought about by those ruling spirits who take over the guidance of mankind every three hundred years. In 1879 Michael took over the rulership, with many of his servants preceding him, preparing for his regency and beginning to develop his style that reached an initial flowering in the Goetheanum. A similar thing took place with his predecessor, Gabriel, during whose rulership the Baroque and Rococo styles developed, and before that the Gothic, the High Gothic. It would be possible to trace these developments in detail according to the various centuries. But what developed at the end of the nineteenth and the beginning of the twentieth century was crowned by the Goetheanum. In the Goetheanum the style we may call Art Nouveau or Jugendstil reached an initial stage of perfection. Herein we should recognize the activity of Michael.

Beyond all the chaos, beyond all the decay, beyond everything that falls away, Michael stands within and above mankind — radiantly — as described in the Michael Meditation. We can unite ourselves with his being by turning to the description that Rudolf Steiner gave of him, by living deeply into this description. Then from this description will stand forth the true picture of the one who is the master builder of our time.

> Michael is a being who actually reveals nothing unless we offer up to him something we have developed ourselves here on earth through diligent spiritual work.

Michael is a silent spirit. Michael is a taciturn spirit.
While the other ruling archangels are talkative spirits —
in a spiritual sense, of course — Michael is altogether
withdrawn, a spirit who speaks little, giving at most
sparse indications. For what we learn from Michael is
not really the word, but — if I may put it that way —
the gaze, the power of his gaze. This is based on the fact
that Michael really occupies himself most of all with
what human beings create out of the spirit. He lives
with the consequences of human actions. The other
spirits live more with the causes; Michael lives more
with the consequences. The other spirits kindle in man
the impulses for what he shall do. Michael will be the
true spiritual hero of freedom. He allows human beings
to act, and then receives what becomes of human deeds
in order to take it further on in the cosmos, in order to
effect through them in the cosmos what human beings
were not yet able to effect.[9]

That is an image of this being. But through the fact that
this being waits and sometimes — in the description of Rudolf
Steiner — interrupts this waiting by beckoning to human beings,
gently prompting them to remember their own spirit nature;
through the fact that this being waits for what we do and not
what we are required or impelled to do, the opportunity is
vouchsafed to us to develop what is most fundamental for our
time: initiative.

The adversary powers are those who want to lift all burdens
from human beings so that they would stagger through day and
night semi-consciously and lost in dreams, leading to the decay
of social structures all around us. To awaken to initiative, on
the other hand, and to form communities out of such initiative
— and within these communities to celebrate Michael festivals
in order to gain fresh impulses and to carry in us the image of
the Goetheanum as the image of the new form of community

— these are the seeds of hope that may prepare the future. Everything else is irrelevant, merely incidental. For what matters today is wherever possible to celebrate the royal wedding, with the worthy and the unworthy, so that the tables may be filled, where the meal of the spirit community may be celebrated. This is the only way of serving Michael.

Appendix

The Social Organism is Threefold

Undated manuscript in English, probably written in 1944

The social organism has three members, it is threefold. Each of these three members is an independent formation, connected with the others and joined to them in manifold ways. And yet we have to study the social structure of each of these three members separately and according to its own laws.

If I study an organism, I first ask myself which are the units that build it up. As the nerve system consists of neurons, the liver of hexagonal liver cells, the muscles of fibres, what — I ask myself — are the units of the social structure? And are they the same for all members, or are there different units for each member?

As everything living consists of cells,

So everything social consists of mankind.

The cell of the social organism, of the body social, is the single human being, who, as a physical-spiritual being has passed through the Fall, bearing bodily form and human individuality.

This human cell, however, is never, or only in rare cases (mental illness) a single, independent being, able to live in this separateness.

Through the mere fact of being human it forms connections to other human beings, or human cells, and, as far as I can see now, this connection which the unit creates for the corresponding social sphere, is a different one for each of the three spheres.

161

The units which form these members of the social organism are:

the human personality	in the free spiritual life,
the family	in the life of rights
the congregation	in the economic life.

Each of these members is more than the mere human being, than the human cell. Each of these units also is more than the human cell, for these units go back to different ancestors

The *human personality* goes back to its own ancestor, its ego, which — created once upon a time — moves from one incarnation to the other carrying its own stream of destiny and its own karma development.

The *family* goes back to the ancestral parents Adam and Eve. It is the family which, especially and specifically, bears the bondage of the Fall and takes care of the continuation of the blood stream and of the powers of heredity.

The *congregation* is a community of single human beings who confess more and more, out of freedom, that not their own karma, nor their body burdened by sin, but something new is at work in the social organism. Their ancestor is not their self, nor Adam and Eve, but Christ chosen in freedom.

In the *free spiritual life*, and only there, the single human individuality comes to expression. Here in learning and teaching in schools and universities, in the give and take of art, in religious contemplation, man finds the expression of his own, personal path.

Karma will ensure that many or some people have the same common striving in this framework. They will combine in associations so that they may give expression to this striving. Thus for instance, an Anthroposophical Society, an association of free artists, a group of people in pursuit of a scientific problem will form their associations. But man is free in these associations. He serves himself and his destiny, for he is the successor of his own ancestor, the ego once created for him.

In the *life of rights*, it is the family which is the determining member. Here father, mother and children form the unit. In the family blood ties and the Fall into sin prevail. The family ensures the continuance of the human species and allows the single human being to receive the body which makes possible his earthly life. The life of rights sees to the rights of the family, and it orders the rights and duties of each of the others; the connections between the families; and those of the families and the single members to the institutions of the spiritual and economic life. The life of rights regulates the wages of the breadwinner of the family; it regulates and guards the right of each member of the family to the free exercise of religious, scientific and artistic opinions and activities. For the building of the Tower of Babel, like the Fall, is preserved through the bond of the family.

In the *economic life,* it is the congregation which permeates it more and more. But here one must differentiate between two things: the organizations of the economic life and the church parishes. The former acts that the latter can evermore unfold their being. The units of the economic organizations are: workshop, factory, shop, farm, mines, fishing boat, means of transport and circulation of money (banks) and various others. These form an interlocking organization which serves neither the single human being, nor the single nation, but all nations, all mankind. There are no state boundaries, only the earth as a whole. The earth as the body of Christ, gives its products — like ore, oil, corn, fruit to the economic life and man tends, trades and distributes these goods all over the earth. In order that this is done in the right way, a common consciousness is needed. But this consciousness can only be created by the congregation. For this process of a growing consciousness can only arise when everyone can partake as an equal of the most precious goods of the earth, bread and wine, as the true body of Christ, in golden or glass vessels; that is when the congregation gathers round the sacrament and becomes the brotherhood of Christ.

Each single human being should grow more and more into a member of these three units. As representative of the economic life he is a member of the congregation of the parish. As a member of the family he is a helper in the life of rights. As bearer of destiny, united with others, he forms the spiritual life.

Man's free individuality, his ego, forms the substance of the spiritual life, here *freedom* must prevail. That means for the created ego: *ex deo nascimur* [we are born from God].

Family, as bearer of the body of sin, handing down the heritage, forms the harmonies which live between human spirit and world spirit, between earth matter and world substance. Man as single individual, must here experience *equality*. For those working in this sphere this means: *in Christo morimur* [we die in Christ]. For only through *in Christo morimur,* can sin be transformed.

The congregation must become the consciousness of the organism as a whole and the foundation of this consciousness is created by the economic life. Here *fraternity*, brotherliness, prevails. As this is a process in the becoming, *per Spiritum Sanctum reviviscimus* [we rise again through the Holy Spirit] sounds through this sphere.

The social organism thereby receives its substance through the individual egos of the human beings living on the earth. That is a process similar to the one which takes place in the human organism in the marrow of the bones. Here the red blood corpuscles are created, there all human egos were once created by the Godhead.

The human egos grow into their earthly bodies in the same way as the erythrocytes (red blood cells) turn into form without nuclei during certain phases. After this soul process of human becoming or the physical process or maturing of the erythrocytes, these stream into the lung, and man is born into his family. As they take in oxygen, so the newborn child the air. From then on the erythrocytes become servants of the metabolism in the lower organism and man becomes bearer of the spiritual life. The erythrocytes become carriers of material precipitation and man becomes the bearer of the economic life. This means that the process of maturing in the erythrocytes corresponds to the process of becoming of the individual ego in his existence between death and a new birth. The red blood corpuscle is then without nucleus. The human individual soul has become ripe for earth life. In the streaming of the marrow to the lung, the embryonic process comes into existence, in the breath of the lung the birth is fulfilled. As the erythrocytes move to and fro through the heart, so the child enters and leaves the family.

As the blood streams into the single organs, so man streams into the branches of spiritual life. In kidneys, liver, spleen, etc. he forms the schools, societies, institutions of learning of the free spiritual life.

Man is born into the family. Here right and equality prevail which are the rhythms of our organism.

We are born out of the spirit. Our skull is the image of the earth, on to which we descend. The brain within the skull is the fully developed economic life and in the centre of the brain is the pineal gland which is kept alive by the especially delicate substances of our food. This is a picture of how the congregation is placed within the economic life: like the pineal gland in our brain. The pineal gland is not outwardly active, but creates consciousness. Thus the congregation surrounding the altar, should not be outwardly active, but create consciousness within the economic life.

Today the head is the only part in man which carries the fully awake consciousness. Therefore the congregations of the Christian church on earth should become the bearers of the fully awake consciousness and thereby the regulator of the social organism. That is their task.

The human ego enters the world through its body. Thus the red blood corpuscle enters the bloodstream from the marrow of the bones.

The ego is born into family. Thus it receives the burden of sin through race and family, and thus the erythrocyte receives its task through the taking in and giving off of oxygen and carbon-dioxide in the realm of the lung.

In the sphere of the free spiritual life man meets his own creative faculties. Here he works as eternal, individual being. In like manner blood flows in the single organs; but there it meets two streams: the ordinary earthly nutrition stream and the cosmic nutrition stream.

Bericht über die Reise nach Böhmen

Wiedersehen mit Prag

Fürstenbühl
am 13. September 1964

I. Das letzte Zusammensein vor dem Sommer,
als ein Bericht über die vergangenen Monate
gegeben wurde, schloß mit dem **Blick**
nach Osten ab.
    Nun ist unser erstes Zusammensein, am
Beginn der Herbstzeit, ein Bericht über
den Besuch in Prag. Ein erster, kleiner
Spalt in der **Türe nach dem Osten** ist
uns geöffnet worden. Es ist zu hoffen, daß
weitere Besuche folgen können.

II. Die Sehnsucht, wieder einmal Böhmen s
Prag besuchen zu können, war groß. Das
schlesisch - böhmische Schicksal.
Die erste heilpädagogische Arbeit in
Pilgramshain.
Die regelmäßigen Besuche in Prag,
Pardubitz, Königgrätz, Olmütz usw.
Die vielen Patienten, die Vorträge, die
einzelnen tschechischen Kinder.

Die Flucht aus Deutschland nach Prag,
Von Prag nach Wien.

Report on the journey to Bohemia
Revisiting Prague

Notes for a Travel Report
Föhrenbühl, September 13, 1964

I.

The final gathering before the summer, at which a report on the preceding months was presented, concluded with a *glance towards the east.*

Now, at the beginning of the autumn season, we will have a report on the visit to Prague. A first, small chink in the *door to the east* has now been opened. The hope is that further visits may follow in the future.

II.

The longing to be able to visit Bohemia and Prague once again was great. Destiny with Silesian-Bohemian.

The early beginnings of curative education in Pilgramshain.

Regular visits to Prague, Pardubitz [Pardubice], Königgrätz [Sadová], Olmütz [Olomouc] etc.

The large number of patients, the lectures, the individual Czech children.

Escape from Germany to Prague. From Prague to Vienna.

Opposite (and following pages): König's notes for his travel report.

2)

III.

Böhmen als ein Herzstück Mitteleuropas.
Sibusa – Přemysl (Prometheus) Přemisliden.
Heiliger Wenzel   28. September 929
Wenzel I, II, III,   Ottokar usw,
Karl IV.   1316 – 1378
     Vorbereitung des Bewußtseins seelen-
     zeitalters.
       Templer – Rosenkreuzer
       Karlstein
       Wenzelskapelle
       Hradschin
Dreißigjähriger Krieg – Chymische Hochzeit
Wallenstein – Ferdinand II
Österreich – Ungarn – Böhmen
Nationalismus   Masaryk
       ↓ |
   Kommunismus   Beneš

IV.

Die Einfahrt ins Land ; Grenzerlebnisse
Die Fahrt nach Prag.
Eger, die Dörfer, die Erde.
Prag
Der Blick auf die Stadt
Karlsbrücke ,
Die Messe in der Teynkirche
Die Wenzelskapelle   Tycho de Brahe
Die Karlsteyn
Die Begegnung mit den Menschen
in den Straßen ∘ Geschäften.

III.

Bohemia as a heart region of Central Europe.
Libuse - Přemysl *(Prometheus)* Přemisliden.
St Wenceslas *September 28, 929*
Wenceslas I, II, III, Otakar etc.
Charles IV 1316–1378

> Preparation of the age of the conscious-
> ness soul
> Templars — Rosicrucians
> Karlstejn
> St Wenceslas' Chapel
> Hradshin (Prague Castle)

Thirty-Years War — Chymical Wedding
Wallenstein — Ferdinand II
Austria — Hungary — Bohemia

Nationalism	Mašaryk
|	|
Communism	Beneš

IV.

Entry into the country; border experiences
Journey to Prague
Eger [Cheb], the villages, the soil
Prague
View of the city
Charles Bridge,
Mass in Tyn Cathedral
St Wenceslas Chapel   Tycho Brahe
Karlstejn [Castle]
Meeting the people
in the streets and shops.

3)

V.

Die Herrschaft der Tyrannen.
Das Hotel
Kongresse.
Die schwarzen Autos

Die Begegnung mit den Freunden.
Die Abgeschlossenheit;
Die Unmöglichkeit geistiger Arbeit.
Die persönliche Not.

Dr Brabниek,
Dr Kroczek,
Pfarrer Adámeč.

VI.

Leipzig kam <u>nicht</u> zustande
Ostdeutschland der nächste Schritt

↲

V.

Rule of the tyrants.
The hotel
Congresses.
The black cars

Meeting with our friends.
The isolation;
The impossibility of spiritual work
Individual problems.

Dr Brabinek
Dr Kroczek
Rev Adamec

VI.

Leipzig did *not* materialize
Eastern Germany the next step

Notes

Introduction

1 Written at Christmas 1938; he had only just fled to London, alone and not knowing how life would go on, or whether family and friends would be able to follow. From König, *Karl König: My Task*, p. 94.

2 From the lecture given on Palm Sunday, March 22, 1964, included in this volume, p. 81.

3 The essay 'Soziale und ökonomische Grundlagen moderner Gemeinschaftsbildung' (social and economic foundations of modern community building) was later published in *Beiträge aus der anthroposophischen Studentenarbeit*, Tübingen, Easter 1966.

4 Essays by Steiner from the magazine *Luzifer-Gnosis*, 1905/6, in *Anthroposophy and the Social Question*.

5 *Was in der anthroposophischen Gesellschaft vorgeht*, Vol. 1, No. 1, Jan 13, 1924. The underlined copy is still in the Karl König Archive in Aberdeen.

6 In König, *The Child with Special Needs*.

7 See facsimile, p. 158

8 See also Steiner, *The Cycle of the Year as a Breathing Process of the Earth.* This motif is elaborated further in Karl König's contemplations on the Anthroposophical Calendar of the Soul, *An Inner Journey through the Year* and *The Calendar of the Soul, a Guide.*

9 'The healthy social life is found when in the mirror of each human soul the whole community finds its reflection and when in the community the virtue of each one is living.' (*Motto of Social Ethics*, inscribed by Rudolf Steiner into a book on the threefold social order, November 1920. In Steiner, *Verses and Meditations*, p.117.)

Motifs of the Social Mission in Karl König's Life

1 Müller-Wiedemann, *Karl König*; König, *Karl König: My Task*, and Selg, *Karl König's Path into Anthroposophy*.

2 Bertha König, *Recollections of my Life*. Bertha König finished her manuscript at Easter 1966, just after the death of her son Karl.

3 Unfortunately this line was omitted in the published English translation.

4 The essays of Anke Weihs and Hans-Heinrich Engel are particularly interesting in this respect; see König, *Karl König, My Task*.

5 Unpublished manuscript, Karl König Archive

6 Steiner, *Innere Entwicklungsimpulse der Menschheit*, lecture of Sep 25, 1916.

7 Selg, *Ita Wegman and Karl König*, pp. 50–59.

8 Extensive texts to this theme are to be found in König, *The Child with Special Needs*.

9 'Autobiographical Fragment' in König, *Karl König: My Task*, p. 41.

10 *The Cresset*, Journal of the Camphill Movement, Michaelmas 1964 (the same time as the lectures published here).

11 'Autobiographical Fragment' in König, *Karl König: My Task*, p. 28.

12 Steiner, *Wahrspruchworte*, p. 269.

13 'König, 'Die drei Leitsterne der Camphill-Bewegung, pp. 9f, quoted in König, *Karl König: My Task*, p. 94.

14 'Inertia of the Heart' was the subtitle that Jakob Wasserman chose for his novel *Kaspar Hauser*.

15 The lecture was published in the journal *Natura*, Arlesheim, No. 3, 1930.

16 This Association was started in Germany through Ita Wegman's initiative in 1928 and she asked König to be a member of board. In the early 30s she ceased such activities due to the political situation and tried to turn people's attention to the coming catastrophe and necessary steps, for instance to get children out of the country.

17 Newsletter of the Independent School for Social Work, No. 1, Eisenach 1932 (in the Karl König Archive).

18 König, *The Child with Special Needs*, p. 41.

19 Letter of Feb 26, 1936, quoted in Selg, *Ita Wegman and Karl König*, p. 60.

20 'Detailed plan for the establishment of an Institution for Curative Education in the South of Ireland' (from the Karl König Archive)

21 'Detailed plan' as above, quoted in König, *Karl König: My Task*, p. 164.

22 *Die Drei*, Stuttgart Vol. 5, No. 29, 1959.

23 See König, *The Child with Special Needs*.

24 König, *Seeds for Social Renewal*, p. 263.

25 König, *The Camphill Movement, Two Essays*.

26 Inauguration of Camphill Hall, Sep 20–22, 1962. Programme and transcript, Karl König Archive.

The Historical Context of the Threefold Social Order

1 Hynes, S. *A War Imagined*, p. 3.

The Spiritual Dimension of Human Development

1 Recently interesting approaches have been found. Raymond Tallis, philosopher and writer is such an example. His book, *I Am: A Philosophical Inquiry*, addresses this subject.

2 König made many studies about the ear. Two of his lectures, held at Christmaas 1949 in Camphill are entitled, *The Human Ear and the Cosmic Word,* there he quotes two lectures by Steiner, *The World of the Senses and the World of the Spirit,* lecture of Jan 1, 1912 and *The Destinies of Individuals and of Nations,* lecture of June 10 1915.

3 Described in Steiner, *Die Mission der neuen Geistesoffenbarung,* lecture of Feb 25, 1911.

Wonder, Compassion and Conscience

1 König probably refers to various remarks Rudolf Steiner had made around 25 years before the 1949 publication of Jaspers' book, the main description being in *Erfahrung des Übersinnlichen,* lecture of May 8, 1912.

2 See Graham Calderwoods work on the heart in the appendix of Edwards, *Vortex of Life.*

3 This was the starting point for König's *Easter Saturday Play,* set at the grave of Golgotha. König mentioned that this play would be important for the work at the Lake of Constance, where the elements of wonder, compassion and love can be experienced as inner qualities in the landscape (see Steel, *Ohn' Mut sind wir nichts).*

4 In *Der irdische und der kosmische Mensch,* lecture of May 14, 1912.

5 Steiner, *The Christmas Conference.*

Developing Responsibility in the Social Realm

1 For instance in *Heilfaktoren für den sozialen Organismus,* Easter lectures of April 2 and 3, 1920, and in *The Inner Aspect of the Social Question,* both of which König certainly used for preparation of these lectures.

2 *Inner Aspect of the Social Question,* lecture of Feb 11, 1919, p. 33f.

3 This and the following three quotations, from *Inner Aspect of the Social Question,* lecture of Feb 11, 1919, pp. 39, 40, 41, 42f.

4 At the end of chapter 26 of his *Autobiography.*

5 *Inner Aspect of the Social Question,* lecture of Feb 11, 1919, p. 46.

The Spiritual History of Central Europe

1 König's preparatory notes for his travel report given at Föhrenbühl a week earlier are in the Archive. See facsimile in the appendix, p. 158, and photograph, p. 8.

2 Polzer-Hoditz, *Erinnerungen an Rudolf Steiner,* p. 98, and Meyer, *Ludwig Polzer-Hoditz.*

3 See also Wegman, *An die Freunde,* p. 124. Regarding the connection of Christian Rosenkreutz with Karlstejn Castle, see Eschborn, *Karlstein.*

4 For example in *Karmic Relationships,* Vol. III, lecture of July 13, 1924.

5 In *Menschenwerden, Weltenseele und Weltengeist,* p. 111, and *Geisteswissenschaft und Medizin,* pp. 180ff and 330.

6 Friend of God was a mystical title in the fourteenth century, which was occasionally attached to the name of Heinrich Seuse (or Suso); in this case the reference is to Tauler's teacher. See Rath, *Der Gottesfreund vom Oberland.*
7 See *Mysterienstätten des Mittelalters,* second lecture, pp. 27ff.
8 See *Mysterienstätten des Mittelalters,* second lecture, p. 46.

The Michael Festival as a New Festival of Community

1 *The Last Address,* p. 18.
2 In *Die menschliche Seele in ihrem Zusammenhang,* p. 189.
3 *Die menschliche Seele in ihrem Zusammenhang,* p. 213.
4 This refers to *Approaching the Mystery of Golgotha,* lectures May 18 and 20, 1913. On May 16 Rudolf Steiner had inspected the site in Dornach and had made the recommendation to the Johannesbauverein to build there. He announced this to the members of the Anthroposophical Society in Stuttgart on May 18. See Lindenberg, *Rudolf Steiner,* p. 536.
5 *The Last Address,* p. 19.

Temple Building and Community Building

1 During the Advent and Christmas season, König gave further lectures in Föhrenbühl, published in *Man as a Social Being.* König's meditative work on the Anthroposophical Soul Calendar constituted the backdrop to these descriptions about the nature and future significance of human conscience for the social realm. At the same time deliberations took place during the winter months about the developing forms of esoteric life of the Camphill community in the future. See also Müller-Wiedemann, *Karl König,* chapter '1964: Charles IV and Karlstejn Castle.'
2 In *Die menschliche Seele in ihrem Zusammenhang,* lecture of May 23, 1923.
3 *The Riddle of Man* was only published in English in 1990, and is only a partial translation. *Riddles of the Soul* was only published in 1996.
4 *Mysterienstätten des Mittelalters.*
5 *Mysterienstätten des Mittelalters,* pp. 89f.
6 On April 23 in the morning Rudolf Steiner gave a lecture for the workers of the Waldorf-Astoria Cigarette Factory in Stuttgart 'Proletarian Demands and their Future Practical Realisation' (in *Neugestaltung des sozialen Organismus).* In the evening he gave the lecture referred to here for members of the Anthroposophical Society; see *Geisteswissenschaftliche Behandlung sozialer und pädagogischer Fragen,* pp. 42f.
7 In November 1965 König then spoke about this in two lectures about euthanasia in Föhrenbühl, published in *The Child with Special Needs.*
8 See incomplete notes in *Wege zu einem neuen Baustil,* p.111.
9 *Mysterienstätten des Mittelalters,* pp. 93f.

Bibliography

Andrae, Johann Valentin, *The Chymical Wedding of Christian Rosenkreutz*, first edition, Strasburg 1616.

Edwards, Lawrence, *The Vortext of Life*, Floris Books 2006.

Eschborn, Michael, *Karlstein*, Stuttgart 1977.

Hynes, S. *A War Imagined, The First World War and English Culture*, London, 1990.

Jaspers, Karl Theodor, *The Origin and Goal of History*, Greenwood Press 1977 (First published in 1949).

König, Bertha, *Recollections of my Life*, Karl König Institute 2010.

König, Karl, *At the Threshold of the Modern Age*, Floris Books 2011.

—, *The Camphill Movement, Two Essays*, Aberdeen 1960.

—, *The Child with Special Needs*, Floris Books 2009

—, *A Christmas Story*, Camphill Books 1995.

—, *Easter Saturday Play,*Camphill Books 1981.

—, *Karl König: My Task*, Floris Books 2008.

—, *A Living Physiology*, Camphill Books 2006.

—, *Man as a Social Being*, Camphill Books 1990.

—, *Seeds for Social Renewal*, Floris Books 2009.

Lindenberg, Christoph, *Rudolf Steiner: eine Biographie*, Stuttgart 1997.

Meyer, Thomas, *Ludwig Polzer-Hoditz: ein Europäer*, Basle 1994.

Müller-Wiedemann, *Karl König, A Central European Biography*, Camphill Press 1996.

Polzer-Hoditz, Ludwig, *Erinnerungen an Rudolf Steiner*, Dornach 1985.

Rath, Wilhelm, *Der Gottesfreund vom Oberland*, Stuttgart 1985.

Rüstow, Alexander, *Freedom and Domination*, Princetown University Press 1980.

Selg, Peter, *Ita Wegman and Karl König*, Floris Books 2008.

—, *Karl König's Path into Anthroposophy*, Floris Books 2008.

Steel, Richard, *Ohn' Mut sind wir nichts: Erika von Arnim zur Erinnerung*, Medical Section, Dornach 2008.

Steiner, Rudolf. Volume Nos. refer to the Collected Works (CW), or to the German Gesamtausgabe (GA)

—, *Anthroposophy and the Social Question*, Mercury Press 1982.

—, *Approaching the Mystery of Golgotha* (CW 152), Steinerbooks, USA 2006.

—, *Architecture as a Synthesis of the Arts* (CW 286), Rudolf Steiner Press, UK 1999.

—, *Autobiography,* SteinerBooks, USA 2006.

—, *Christianity as Mystical Fact,* Rudolf Steiner Publications, New York 1961.

—, *The Christmas Conference for the Foundation of the General Anthroposophical Society 1923-1924,* Anthroposophic Press 1990.

—, *Cosmic Memory,* Harper and Row 1981.

—, *The Cycle of the Year as Breathing Process of the Earth* (CW 223), Anthroposophic Press, USA 1988.

—, *The Destinies of Individuals and of Nations* (CW 157), Anthroposophic Press, USA 1987.

—, *Earthly and Cosmic Man* (CW 133), Rudolf Steiner Publishing, London 1948.

—, *Erfahrung des Übersinnlichen: die Wege der Seele zu Christus* (GA 143), Dornach 1994.

—, *Geisteswissenschaft als Erkenntnis der Grundimpulse sozialer Gestaltung (GA 199),* Dornach 1985 (English: *Spiritual Science as Foundation for Social Forms).*

—, *Geisteswissenschaft und Medizin* (GA 312), Dornach 1999 (English: *Introducing Anthroposophical Medicine).*

—, *Geisteswissenschaftliche Behandlung sozialer und pädagogischer Fragen* (GA 192) Dornach 1991.

—, *Heilfaktoren für den sozialen Organismus* (GA 198), Dornach 1994.

—, *The Inner Aspect of the Social Question* (CW 193), Rudolf Steiner Press, UK 1974.

—, *Innere Entwicklungsimpulse der Menschheit* (GA 171), Dornach 1984.

—, *Introducing Anthroposophical Medicine* (CW 312), Anthroposophic Press, USA 1999).

—, *Intuitive Thinking as a Spiritual Path: A Philosophy of Freedom* (CW 4), Anthroposophic Press, USA 1995.

—, *Der irdische und der kosmische Mensch (GA 133),* Dornach 1989 (English: *Earthly and Cosmic Man).*

—, *Der Jahreskreislauf als Atmungsprozess der Erde* (GA 223), Dornach 1990.

—, *Karmic Relationships,* Vol. III, (CW 237), Rudolf Steiner Press, UK 1977.

—, *Karmic Relationships,* Vol. IV, (CW 238), Rudolf Steiner Press, UK 1977.

—, *The Last Address,* Rudolf Steiner Press, UK 1967.

—, *Menschenwerden, Weltenseele und Weltengeist,* Vol. I, GA 205, Dornach 1987.

—, *Die menschliche Seele in ihrem Zusammenhang mit göttlich-geistigen Individualitäten* (GA 224), Dornach 1992.

—, *Die Mission der neuen Geistesoffenbarung* (GA 127), Dornach 1989.

—, *Mysterienstätten des Mittelalters. Rosenkreuzertum und modernes Einweihungsprinzip* (GA 233a), Dornach 1991.

—, *Neugestaltung des sozialen Organismus* (GA 330), Dornach 1883.

—, *The Philosophy of Freedom* (CW 4), Anthroposophic Press, USA 1964 (New edition: *Intuitive Thinking as a Spiritual Path*).

—, *The Riddle of Man* (part of CW 20) Mercury Press, USA 1990.

—, *Riddles of the Soul* (CW 21), Mercury Press, USA 1996.

—, *Spiritual Science as a Foundation for Social Forms* (CW 199), Anthroposophic Press, USA 1986.

—, *Verses and Meditations,* Rudolf Steiner Press, UK 1972.

—, *Vom Menschenrätsel* (GA 20), Dornach 1984 (English: *The Riddle of Man*).

—, *Von Seelenrätseln* (GA 21), Dornach 1983 (English: *Riddles of the Soul*).

—, *Vorstufen zum Mysterium von Golgatha* (GA 152), Dornach 1990 (English: *Approaching the Mystery of Golgotha*).

—, *Wahrspruchworte* (GA 40), Dornach 2005.

—, *Wege zu einem neuen Baustil* (GA 286), Dornach 1982 (English: *Architecture as a Synthesis of the Arts*).

—, *The World of the Senses and the World of the Spirit* (CW 134) Rudolf Steiner Publishing Co, London 1947.

Tallis, Raymond, *I Am: A Philosophical Inquiry into First-Person Being,* Edinburgh University Press 2004.

—, *Michelangelo's Finger — an Exploration of Everyday Transcendence,* Atlantic Books, London 2010.

Tetens, Johannes Nikolaus, *Philosophische Versuche über die menschliche Natur und ihre Entwickelung,* 2 volumes, Leipzig 1777.

Wegman, Ita, *An die Freunde,* Arlesheim 1960.

Index

Albertus Magnus 118f, 122
Anaximander 92
Annas 96
Anthroposophical Society 14
Aristotle 75
Arras, Matthias of see Matthias of
  Arras
Art Nouveau 156f

Baden, Crown Prince of 47
Baer, Karl Ernst von 65
Bauhaus 156
Black Death see plague
Blue Rider 156
Boccaccio, Giovanni 118, 120
Bock, Emil 32, 35
Bockholt, Dr 29
Bolshevism 66
Brabinek, Dr 8
Brachenreuthe Camphill Com-
  munity 15
Brentano, Franz 147
Bucknall, Morwenna 25
Buddha 92

Caesar, Julius 91
Caiaphas 96
Camphill Hall 39–41
'Candle on the Hill' 26
Cato, Marcus Porcius (the Younger)
  91
centralized state 50, 52, 60–62, 103
Charles IV 115, 117f, 121f, 125f,
  128–130, 139

Christ 105–8
Chymical Wedding 116
Clémenceau, Georges 54f
Cold War 66
colonialism 51, 55, 60, 62
Comenius, Amos 41
compassion 94
Confucius 92
conscience 92–94, 96
Copernicus, Nicolaus 49

Dante 118f
Darwinism 65
Dessoir, Max 147
Doldinger, Friedrich 32

ear 80
Easter 17
Easter Saturday 96
Eckhart, Meister 122
Eisenach 32
Elijah 132
Elisabeth of Hungary, St 32
Engels, Friedrich 64
erythrocytes (red blood cells) 164f
Eschenbach, Wolfram von 32

Fascism 66
Fichte, Immanuel Hermann 147
Fichte, Johann Gottlieb 147
First World War 65
Föhrenbühl Camphill School 15, 16
Franz Ferdinand, Archduke 54
Freemason 137

French Revolution 63
Friend of God 122f

Galileo Galilei 49
Gaulle, Charles de 54, 57, 62
Geoffroy Saint-Hilaire, Étienne 67
George, David Lloyd see Lloyd
  George, David
Goethe, Johann Wolfgang von 65, 67
Goetheanum 39, 134, 138, 143–45,
  148, 150, 153
Golden Bull 125f, 129, 139
Good Friday 96
Grazie, Eugenie delle 156
Grey, Sir Edward 54

Haeckel, Ernst 150
Hauptmann, Gerhart 156
hearing 80
Hegel, G.W.F. 147
Henry VIII 51
Heraclitus 92
Herder, Johann Gottfried von 65, 67
human organism, threefold 68
Hundred Years War 62
Hus, Jan 121

Independent College for Social Work
  32, 35
Industrial Revolution 63, 65

Jaspers, Karl 92
Jehovism 103
Jerome of Prague 121
Joan of Arc 62
John the Baptist 132
John the Evangelist 132
Joseph of Arimathea 96, 97

Karlstejn Castle 41, 115–17, 126–30,
  138, 151
Kepler, Johannes 49
Klimt, Gustav 156
König, Bertha 20
König, Karl 2, 35
—, death 16

König, Tilla (née Mathilde Maasberg)
  29
Kühlmann, Richard von (German
  Foreign Minister) 47

labour 53
Lamarck, Jean-Baptiste 67
language 81, 89f
Lassalle, Ferdinand 64
Lazarus 132
Lloyd George, David 54f
Logos 140f
Louis XIV 61
Ludmilla, St 116, 128
Luther, Martin 51

Mahler, Gustav 156
Maillol, Aristide 156
Marx, Karl 64, 138
Mathilde Maasberg see König, Tilla
Matthias of Arras 117
Maundy Thursday 95f
mechanization 50
memory 90
Michael, Archangel 133–35, 138,
  142, 157–159
Michaelmas 17, 136f, 142, 144f
Molay, Jacques de 129
Morris, William 156
Munch, Edvard 156

Napoleon 61
nationalism 61, 103
National Socialism 66
Nicodemus 96f
Nolde, Emil 156
Novalis 133

Owen, Robert 13, 25, 41, 64

Paracelsus (Theophrastus Bombastus
  von Hohenheim) 67
Parler, Peter 117
Petrarch, Francesco 118, 120
Philip the Fair 61, 129
Pietzner, Carlo 8

Pilate 96
Pilgramshain 29
plague (Black Death) 119f
Planck, Karl Christian 147
Poincaré, Raymond 54
Poltzer-Hoditz, Count and Countess 115
Preuss, Wilhelm Heinrich 147
Pythagoras 92

Raphael 133
Riddle of Man, The 146f
Riddles of the Soul 146–48
Rosenkreutz, Christian 129f
Rosicrucian, Rosicrucianism 124, 129, 139, 149
Roth, Alix 8
Rüstow, Alexander 49

Saint-Hilaire, Geoffroy *see* Geoffroy Saint-Hilaire, Étienne
Schelling, Friedrich Wilhelm Joseph 147
Schiele, Egon 156
sense of I 79f, 83
sense of thought 79f, 83
sense of word 78, 80, 82
Seuse (or Suso), Heinrich 122
Socialist International 138

Steiner, Rudolf 29, 47, 92, 101, 105, 115, 131
Stein, Walter Johannes 30
Strohschein, Albrecht 29
Suso, Heinrich *see* Seuse, Heinrich
Switzerland 125

Taoism 92
Tauler, Johannes 122f
Templar, Knights 22, 61, 129
Tetens, Johannes Nikolaus 67
Teutonic Knights, Order of 118, 125
Theodoric of Prague 128
Thirty Years War 52
Thomas Aquinas 118f, 122
Titanic 54

Velde, Henry van der 156

Wartburg 32
Wegman, Ita 26, 29f, 32
Wenceslas, St 115, 128
Wilson, Woodrow 54f
Wycliffe, John 120f

Zarathustra 122
Zhuangzi 92
Zinzendorf, Count Ludwig 29, 41
zoön politikon 75f

Karl König's collected works are being published in English by Floris Books, Edinburgh and in German by Verlag Freies Geistesleben, Stuttgart. They are issued by the Karl König Archive, Aberdeen in co-operation with the Ita Wegman Institute for Basic Research into Anthroposophy, Arlesheim. They seek to encompass the entire, wide-ranging literary estate of Karl König, including his books, essays, manuscripts, lectures, diaries, notebooks, his extensive correspondence and his artistic works. The publications will fall into twelve subjects.

The aim is to open up König's work in a systematic way and make it accessible. This work is supported by many people in different countries.

Overview of Karl König Archive subjects

Medicine and study of the human being
Curative education and social therapy
Psychology and education
Agriculture and science
Social questions
The Camphill movement
Christianity and the festivals
Anthroposophy
Spiritual development
History and biographies
Artistic and literary works
Karl König's biography

Karl König Archive
Camphill House
Milltimber
Aberdeen AB13 0AN
United Kingdom
www.karl-koenig-archive.net
aberdeen@karl-koenig-archive.net

Ita Wegman Institute for Basic
Research into Anthroposophy
Pfeffingerweg 1a
4144 Arlesheim
Switzerland
www.wegmaninstitut.ch
koenigarchiv@wegmaninstitut.ch